As the pace of change accelerates, navigating change in the competitive marketplace has never been more important. This book presents a primer on the state of the art of best practices in coaching and provides tools to chart the course. It is a treasure trove of information to help you understand the challenges, what gets in the way, what's at stake, and the opportunity of what is possible when change is approached in a thoughtful, strategic, people-centered manner. Bravo!

Carole Dickert-Scherr, former vice president, Human Resources, PBS

Building the Core Competencies of Change should be required reading, not only for those in the C-suite, but for employees at all levels. Sandi Stewart is one of the finest coaches I've encountered in my four decades of professional experience. In *Building the Core Competencies of Change*, Sandi shares highlights from her rich trove of experience and ties what she's learned to easily understood, actionable items for the reader. Sandi's personal warmth and humility are apparent throughout, making *Building the Core Competencies of Change* a fun and fast read. Whether you read it in one sitting or a chapter at a time over a longer period, you will want to keep this valuable resource close at hand so you can refer back to it over and over as you navigate the quickening pace of change in the twenty-first century workplace.

Bob Fleshner, former CEO, UnitedHealthcare of the Mid-Atlantic

Building the Core Competencies of Change is a timely, powerful guide for leaders to use the techniques of coaching to support change in their organizations. It is particularly relevant in the current environment, where organizations and the people who work in them need to adapt to evolving demands in their marketplaces and workforces. The book is clear, practical, and easy to read. Sandi brings her wealth of coaching experience to illustrate key concepts and provide a guide to understanding and applying coaching. A great resource for executives looking to raise the performance of their organizations in a time of change.

Christine Yamamoto, former Americas Tax Practice talent leader, Ernst & Young, LLP

Coaching programs for leaders in higher education have the power to build capacity for change that is very much in demand at today's academic institutions. As traditional models evolve to meet needs in a volatile, uncertain, complex, and ambiguous world, the competencies of flexibility, resilience, and a growth mindset have become the gateway to fulfilling the university's mission to society. The approaches and benefits of coaching programs outlined in Sandi's work detail the elements that enable college and university faculty and administrators to form the communities of innovation that will create the future state of higher education in the US.

Sheila Way, director, HR Processes and Human Resources, American University

I highly recommend this book to everyone who has an interest in leadership coaching and organizational growth. Sandi is an amazing, transformational coach and leader. Her ability to listen and see the deeper issues in every situation is what eventually brings forth lasting change and positive growth for people and organizations.

Dr. Nick Sarantopoulos, president and CEO, Community Credit Union

Sandi Stewart's keen insights into coaching have helped organizations of all kinds develop leaders and unlock untapped value. Her model for building the core competencies of change inspired a critical portion of my doctoral dissertation focused on strengthening nonprofit board governance through the strategic use of coaching and coaching skills.

Dr. Christopher Currens, federal training officer, executive coach, leadership development consultant

Coaching has evolved over the past two decades from an intervention designed to unlock individual potential to a strategic tool to create competitive advantage for organizations. Sandi Stewart offers compelling insights and actionable steps with refreshing personal honesty and present-day examples that will help companies and leaders unleash the power of coaching in organizational transformation.

Christopher Brookfield, principal, Heidrick & Struggles; director, Leadership Coaching for Organizational Performance

I am thrilled to have a resource that clearly defines the organizational benefits of coaching and outlines strategic models for success. In her coaching and through this book, Sandi shares how to develop competencies of change and explains the importance of values and emotions. I admire Sandi's ability to help others understand the opportunities for change and translate those into meaningful organizational and personal goals. This book is definitely a must-read for leading change and embracing the benefits of coaching!

Jacqueline Basile, vice president and Chief Human Resources Officer, The Brookings Institution

This book is a must-read for those who want future-ready organizations where personal fulfillment and organizational performance harmoniously produce results. The social contract between employee and employer is evolving, and *Building the Core Competencies of Change* provides wisdom, expertise, and advice for leaders and organizational influencers on how to successfully navigate this change. The book provides proven frameworks and tools that can equip leaders with the mindsets, behaviors, and sense of purpose to guide and, most importantly, ignite change.

Dr. Philipia Hillman, vice president, Talent and Client Experience, THRUUE

Sandra Stewart has drawn on her extensive experience as a coach and consultant to create a comprehensive overview of how to integrate coaching into organizational strategy. She demonstrates how organizations can move toward a more open and curious mindset that thrives in change. Her detailed summary of the various types, tools, and models of coaching informs how to develop a comprehensive and effective program to support an organization's most crucial resource: its people.

Kathy Taberner, coauthor, *The Power of Curiosity: How to Have Real Conversations that Create Collaboration, Innovation and Understanding*

BUILDING

THE

CORE COMPETENCIES

of

CHANGE

BUILDING THE CORE COMPETENCIES

of

CHANGE

A GUIDE TO
COACHING IN ORGANIZATIONS

Sandra L. Stewart

Published by Advantage, Charleston, South Carolina.
Member of Advantage Media Group.

ADVANTAGE is a registered trademark, and the Advantage colophon is a trademark of Advantage Media Group, Inc.

Printed in the United States of America.

10 9 8 7 6 5 4 3 2 1

ISBN: 978-1-64225-253-8
LCCN: 2021914274

Cover design by George Stevens.
Layout design by Carly Blake.

This publication is designed to provide accurate and authoritative information in regard to the subject matter covered. It is sold with the understanding that the publisher is not engaged in rendering legal, accounting, or other professional services. If legal advice or other expert assistance is required, the services of a competent professional person should be sought.

 Advantage Media Group is proud to be a part of the Tree Neutral® program. Tree Neutral offsets the number of trees consumed in the production and printing of this book by taking proactive steps such as planting trees in direct proportion to the number of trees used to print books. To learn more about Tree Neutral, please visit **www.treeneutral.com**.

Advantage Media Group is a publisher of business, self-improvement, and professional development books and online learning. We help entrepreneurs, business leaders, and professionals share their Stories, Passion, and Knowledge to help others Learn & Grow. Do you have a manuscript or book idea that you would like us to consider for publishing? Please visit **advantagefamily.com**.

To my children and lifelong teachers, Ali and Dash.
And to my supportive husband, Michael.

CONTENTS

INTRODUCTION 1

ANNOTATED TABLE OF CONTENTS 5

DEFINITIONS 9

CHAPTER 1 15
Coaching for Optimizing Organizations, Building Competitive Advantage, and Enhancing Societal Change

CHAPTER 2 39
Emotions and Values in the Workplace

CHAPTER 3 55
The Human Challenge in Change

CHAPTER 4 75
Human Challenge Coaching: More Than Behavioral Change

CHAPTER 5 95
The Seven Competencies of Human Challenge Coaching

CHAPTER 6 125
Coaching in Organizations:
The Seven Factors for Effective Coaching in Organizations

CHAPTER 7 . . . . **143**
Seven Coaching Types for Organizations

CHAPTER 8 . . . . **159**
Techniques and Technology Tools for Aligning
Coaching to Organization Outcomes

CHAPTER 9 . . . . **177**
Coaching Program Impact Models and Examples

CHAPTER 10 . . . . **195**
Putting It in Action:
The Coaching Program Strategy

CHAPTER 11 . . . . **225**
Looking into the Future

APPENDIX **239**

ENDNOTES **241**

ACKNOWLEDGMENTS **245**

ABOUT THE AUTHOR **247**

Those quoted in this book are change-makers.
They make change through their poetry, their music,
their words, and their lives. This one is from me:

Let your life be your art.
Let your art be your purpose.
Let your purpose be your life.

INTRODUCTION

"Change is the only constant in life."

—HERACLITUS, PHILOSOPHER

W hy not start with a confession? I like my habits. I like to feel in control of my environment, and I don't like to look stupid. When I don't know something or make a mistake in public, it can evoke a sense of shame. As a ruminator, I can review past actions over and over in my head—to the point of agonizing—as I think about what I did and what I should have done.

And I admit I have felt a prisoner of my own habits. I couldn't see other choices in front of me or believe that I had the power or capability to make a different choice. Some opportunities in life were just not available to me—at least so I thought, and frankly still continue to think, consciously or unconsciously.

It is hard to engage in the human process of learning and break out of old patterns. It is difficult to see and believe that there are other choices and possibilities. It's not easy to have the courage to try something different that might or might not work.

I am not alone in this. In my over twenty years as a coach and coach instructor, I have had the privilege of playing a role in the exponential growth and change that clients have made in their work and personal lives. This reminds me again and again that we can all continue to grow, learn, and strive to be better people throughout our lives.

Of course, that doesn't mean it is easy. Through coaching, I have found a way to help others make their way through change, growth, and learning a bit easier and faster. Personally, it has taught me to be a better learner by understanding my reactions to change and then funneling my emotions into forward movement instead of procrastination or avoidance.

Once we better understand our reactions to change, we are open to more possibility. Coaching gives us choices: choices in how we think about our experience and how we react to it. These choices create the opportunity to unleash our human potential in areas where we may have felt it was limited. The choices can also enhance our sense of ourselves and our life's purpose. When we are freed from a fear-based mindset, we can make choices that benefit not just ourselves and our organizations but also humanity.

In this book, I hope to provide an understanding of the basic difficulties change presents for all of us and how coaching can help us to overcome these and catalyze positive forward momentum. It is a book to help leaders of organizations to engender the power of change in their people, and therefore their organizations, through coaching. I provide a resource of coaching definitions, tools, and processes to inform executives, talent management professionals, and coaches in a creative and strategic approach to applying coaching.

In the following chapters I outline frameworks to understand the diverse ways coaching can be deployed. Then I lay out the process to build strategic coaching programs. Used correctly, these programs will leverage human potential in organizations to achieve strategic objectives.

While the pages collectively portray a comprehensive look at the power of coaching for organizations and society, you may find some sections more applicable to your areas of interest. I suggest a review of the Annotated Table of Contents to target your reading; however, I recommend the first five chapters to understand change and coaching as the foundation for the rest of the book. As reference, chapters 1 through 5 cover why change is so hard and how coaching works as well as coaching's benefits to individuals and organizations. Chapters 6 through 8 look at how coaching can effectively be used within organizations by defining the types and tools currently available in building a coaching program. Chapters 9 and 10 explore how to deploy a coaching program within an organization. Chapter 11 widens the lens to consider the global benefits of coaching and the future of coaching in organizations and even society.

This book can serve multiple audiences in different ways:

For all of us to understand:

- ✓ Why change is so hard

- ✓ How to build your capacity for change

- ✓ Coaching and what makes it powerful

- ✓ How to build the competencies of change in your organization

Executives and talent development professionals to learn:

- ✓ How to create a culture to succeed in this fast-paced, changing marketplace

- ✓ How to build competitive advantages with the core competencies of change in your people

✓ How to build a strategic coaching program to achieve organizational goals

✓ The diverse types of coaching tools, types, and models that can be deployed for coaching programs

✓ Examples of coaching programs from around the world

Coaches and aspiring coaches to learn:

✓ The key skills to coach powerfully with the Human Challenge

✓ The factors for successful coaching in organizations

✓ How to align coaching to organizational goals

✓ How coaching transforms organizations as well as individuals and teams

✓ How coaching is making change in society as a whole

ANNOTATED TABLE OF CONTENTS

Introduction

Recognize the challenges inherent in change. Learn how coaching can be used to help optimize human potential and drive organizational outcomes. Observe and consider how coaching is now poised to help create and support change within individuals and organizations.

Chapter 1: Coaching for Optimizing Organizations, Building Competitive Advantage, and Enhancing Societal Change

View the power and potential of coaching. Recognize how it has evolved and understand the core competencies of change created by coaching. See how organizations use coaching to build cultures that thrive in change.

Chapter 2: Emotions and Values in the Workplace

The way we deal with emotions is changing within organizations. To understand this, review input from thought leaders. Then consider how the organizations that foster learning can address emotions and change. Learn the importance of values in the workplace and how they can drive motivation or inhibit taking action.

Chapter 3: The Human Challenge in Change

Learn the full definition of the phrase "Human Challenge." Recognize how it presents itself within organizations. Evaluate its relationship to generative learning, as well as the concepts of a fixed mindset and a growth mindset.

Chapter 4: Human Challenge Coaching: More Than Behavioral Change

Learn how coaching for the Human Challenge creates sustainable change in both behavior and mindset. Recognize how this form of coaching is different from a more tactical approach.

Chapter 5: The Seven Competencies of Human Challenge Coaching

Observe how Human Challenge coaching uses seven competencies to unleash human potential. Think about what each one of these competencies involves, and how it can be applied to individuals, teams, and organizations. Engage in self-exploration with demonstration exercises.

Chapter 6: Coaching in Organizations: The Seven Factors for Effective Coaching in Organizations

Recognize what's needed to have powerful coaching in organizations. See how implementing these seven factors can lead to changes that last for clients and their organizations.

Chapter 7: Seven Coaching Types for Organizations

Review the different types of coaching available to build a coaching program. Learn how coaching can be carried out to optimize individual performance, enhance teamwork, and teach leaders and managers coaching skills.

Chapter 8: Techniques and Technology Tools for Aligning Coaching to Organization Outcomes

Learn about alignment meetings and 360 feedback techniques to see their importance in coaching in organizations to align with organization goals. View some of today's innovative technology tools that help take coaching to the next level within organizations.

Chapter 9: Coaching Program Impact Models and Examples

Learn about the three impact models of coaching programs: Individual-Target, Audience-Target, and Organization-Target. Along with understanding how they work, see them in action in different organizations.

Chapter 10: Putting It in Action: The Coaching Program Strategy

There are eleven steps to achieve desired organizational outcomes with coaching. Observe what they are, how they can be implemented, and how they are used in organizations today.

Chapter 11: Looking into the Future

See how organizations are integrating coaching into their products and services to enhance customer attraction and retention. Review how coaching embeds the core competencies of change. Learn how the ICF Ignite program has successfully used coaching to transform society with a focus on education in countries around the globe. Think about what's ahead for coaching, our organizations, and our world.

Appendix

Access resources related to coaching in organizations at QR Code and link: www.corecompetenciesofchange.com.

DEFINITIONS

These are the definitions of terms that appear throughout the book.

Coaching

Coaching is defined as partnering with clients in a thought-provoking and creative process that inspires them to maximize their personal and professional potential through generative learning and knowledge building. When coaching is most powerful, it accesses emotions, values, and mindsets, which are the bedrock of growth and change. "Human Challenge" coaching in this book refers to the powerful coaching achieved in bringing awareness to underlying emotions, values, and mindsets.

Coaching in Organizations or Organizational Coaching

Coaching individuals and teams that work for an organization. The coaching is generally funded by the organization.

The Human Challenge

The Human Challenge is our understanding and working with our sense of self and our human qualities. The Human Challenge is the challenge to be able to recognize and articulate our own emotions, values, beliefs, and mindsets through introspective reflection and then to be able to use them to make choices rather than to engage in habitual response. When we articulate our emotions and values, we can uncover mental models and mindsets that we carry both consciously and unconsciously. These mindsets, once seen, can then be observed as choices rather than presumptions. Once we see that our mindset is a choice, it opens more alternatives to us in how we see ourselves and our limitations and opportunities. The Human Challenge exists not just on an individual level but also on a team or group level, an organization level, and even a societal level, as groups of individuals create mindsets and adopt beliefs that create the culture lens through which they collectively see the world.

The Core Competencies of Change

Coaching, at its best, builds the competencies of change. It helps to develop people's resiliency to change and to move proactively forward. The competencies include:

- The Open Mind—the ability to adopt new information and ideas

- The Curious Mind—the ability to challenge assumptions and the status quo and ask powerful questions

- The Optimistic Mind—the ability to think in terms of possibility and overcome hopelessness

- The Self-Aware Mind—the ability to explore and understand the self to better manage one's choices and impact on others

- The Other-Aware Mind—the ability to understand others

- The Values-Driven Spirit—the ability to align with purpose consistent with one's values

Coaching Types, Models, and Tools

Types of Coaching

These are the different ways coaching is used depending on the type of recipient and how the coaching skills are deployed. Seven of the main types are: individual optimization, individual development and performance, team optimization, team work content, coaching skills training and use, group coaching, and peer coaching.

Coaching Tools

These are tools deployed to align coaching engagements to goals and to support and manage coaching engagements.

Coaching Models

The coaching models are Individual-Target, Audience-Target, and Organization-Target. Each model has a different level of impact and scope. As such, the amount of oversight and top leadership involvement required will vary, depending on which model is used.

Coaching Program Strategist (CPS)

The coaching program strategist is a professional inside or outside the organization who creates the strategic plan for the coaching integration with business objectives. The internal CPS may be the chief human resources officer, chief talent leader, or an HR professional. External to the organizations, the CPS may be a professional in a coach-scaling organization, change management consultancy, or a professional coach with strategy skills. The CPS is instrumental in designing a program that may include different types, tools, and models of coaching in one initiative. Due to the high-level strategic impact of this model, the executive leadership is often engaged.

Coach Program Manager (CPM)

The Coach Program Manager may not have the strategic expertise of the CPS. The CPM focuses on the overall coaching program management. They may design coaching engagements and then oversee the coordination and quality control processes.

Coach-Scaling Organization (CSO)

A coach-scaling organization is an organization that provides external coaches at scale to organizations by vetting a roster of coaches that the client organization can access. They have a technology system that tracks the coaching engagements. Some CSOs also provide a strategic consulting approach at the design phase of a coaching engagement.

Generative Learning and the Learning Loop

Generative learning is where learning takes place in an iterative process of trying and revising actions to continue to refine the object of learning. Learning to play a sport is a generative learning process, as opposed to rote learning of the capitals of each country.

CHAPTER 1

Coaching for Optimizing Organizations, Building Competitive Advantage, and Enhancing Societal Change

---

"The person who figures out how to harness
the collective genius of the people in his or her
organization is going to blow the competition away."
—WALTER WRISTON, FORMER CEO OF CITIBANK

---

n today's dynamic economic and political environment, an organization's success is built on people with the capability to manage through change. Since people are the foundation of change, the leadership of change isn't simply about turning a knob on a machine or a quick behavior modification exercise. It's about helping people to think and learn differently. It's about mitigating people's fears and leveraging their passion and connection to purpose. We must empower people to think agilely and take on new mindsets, as well as understand and solve problems from creative points of view.

Coaching creates the core competencies required for change: an open and curious mindset, self-awareness and understanding of others, and the ability to connect to values that motivate and create optimism. It is essentially a process of building the ability to learn and overcome internal and external barriers that get in the way of growth. We are discovering that the most effective way to leverage human potential is to integrate coaching and coaching mindsets into individuals and organization culture.

When coaching is used strategically to support desired initiatives and organizational outcomes, it becomes a powerful lever to break down barriers to change.

Every organizational initiative is led, driven, and supported by people, but it can also be blocked, thwarted, and resisted by people. When coaching is used strategically to support desired initiatives and organizational outcomes, it becomes a powerful lever to break down barriers to change. It can open up creativity, positivity, and empowerment for people at all levels of an organization. Coaching in all its forms—individual, team, and organizational—can be effective in facilitating the speed of innovation, change, and growth. However, as long as we only see coaching as a simple tactic, we will not fully realize its power to unlock the full potential of our people to achieve sustainable change.

The purpose of this book is to look at coaching through a strategic lens. We'll consider the role coaching plays in organizational change and achieving organizational outcomes. When done well, it can create competitive advantages and leave a lasting imprint on the organization, its people, and its performance.

In this chapter, I'll explain the reasoning behind using coaching strategically. I'll outline how coaching has evolved in a way that is similar to how technology has evolved inside organizations, and how it now has the power to create competitive advantages. I'll also touch on how coaching can expand beyond a single organization and create benefits for society.

HOW COACHING HAS GROWN WORLDWIDE

The coaching of executives, leaders, and managers in organizations has become widespread during the previous two decades. Businesses, nonprofits, and governments employ coaches around the globe. According to the 2020 ICF Global Coaching Study, there were approximately seventy-one thousand coach practitioners in 2019, an increase of 33 percent from 2015.[1]

The estimated global total revenue from coaching in 2019 was 2.8 billion US dollars, representing a 21 percent increase over the 2015 estimate. Growth was especially strong in the emerging regions of Latin America and the Caribbean (+174 percent) and Eastern Europe (+40 percent). The number of managers and leaders using coaching skills is estimated to have risen by almost half (+46 percent) since 2015. The International Coach Federation now has over thirty-six thousand certified members in 145 countries.[2]

Access resources related to coaching in organizations at QR Code and link: linktr.ee/sandrastewart.

EVOLUTION OF COACHING: FROM TACTICAL TOOL TO STRATEGICALLY ALIGNED PROGRAMS

I have coached individuals and teams in hundreds of organizations since 1999. When I started in the profession, organizations were generally hiring coaches one at a time, in a one-off fashion to remedy difficult employee situations as a last-ditch attempt at "fixing" someone. Quickly, organizations found the expense of a coach was wasted on the outgoing employees and began to shift focus to their high performers that, when coached, could deliver exponential value back to the organization.

With the maturation of coaching, new types, tools, and models of coaching have expanded the way organizations can apply coaching. Organizations are now discovering the power of coaching not just for individuals but also to deliver desired organizational outcomes and to build competitive advantage in an important era of market complexity and fast-paced change. With the integration of coaching, talent development efforts are building core competencies that foundationally change the way people think, grow, and innovate. This ability to meet change quickly and creatively creates a competitive edge in the fast-changing marketplace.

Organizations now use coaching to make internal organizational changes of all kinds to expedite the adoption of new systems, structures, and strategies. Recent trends in coaching demonstrate that coaching also adds value to product and service offerings, resulting in competitive advantages that increase revenue and customer loyalty.

Coaching is growing into a strategic tool for organizational outcomes.

COACHING INDUSTRY GROWTH PATH MIMICS THAT OF TECHNOLOGY

In a broad sense, the evolution of information technology from tactical tool to revenue-generating products and services can provide a model for how coaching is evolving today. Like the evolution of IT, coaching has moved from a tactical tool through the stages of improving a system and to creating core competencies for competitive market advantage into new sources of revenue. Today, 10 percent of the US GDP comes from technology service and product companies.[4] Coaching has the similar potential to transform marketplace opportunities.

IT

COACHING

I

IMPROVE A SINGLE PROCESS

Automate a spreadsheet

IMPROVE A SINGLE PERSON

Optimize a single leader's performance

II

IMPROVE A SYSTEM

Automate a financial reporting system

IMPROVE MULTIPLE PEOPLE'S PERFORMANCE

Optimize a restructuring or culture change through addressing the Human Challenge with coaching

III

BUILD A COMPETITIVE CORE COMPETENCY

Create speed to market with technology

BUILD A COMPETITIVE CORE COMPETENCY

Create speed to market with a core competency culture of innovation and change

IV

BUILD BETTER PRODUCTS FOR MARKET SUPERIORITY

Integrate technology into products and services

BUILD BETTER PRODUCTS FOR MARKET SUPERIORITY

Integrate coaching with your products and services

V

BUILD A NEW BUSINESS

Sell to consumers the technology solution you developed for your operations

BUILD A NEW BUSINESS

Sell to consumers a coaching product or service you developed for your operations

IT and coaching have followed similar evolutionary paths.

Thinking back to the beginning of the IT transformation, the first computers were used as tools to crunch data at faster rates. Later, technology transformed processes like financial reporting, product and service delivery, and employee management systems.

As technical innovations sped up and improved business operations, computers moved from being a tactical tool to a strategic lever. Now, computers could do more than add and subtract; they could improve a company's performance. Businesses that operated faster gained advantages over their slower or less innovative competitors. Organizations that adopted IT early and elevated their IT strategy into the executive suite became market leaders.

Eventually, executives realized their technology could be packaged and sold to customers. As a result, these new product lines created new sources of revenue.

Technology created such profound competitive advantages that it disrupted entire industries.

Today, computing and information technology are fundamental to how we operate in the world. They are both a facilitator of the business operations and part of the very product that businesses sell. Whole industries are built on technology.

In much the same way that IT transformed organizations, coaching has grown from being viewed as a simple tool. As I mentioned earlier, during the infancy of coaching, organizations deployed coaching tactically to mitigate issues created by "problem" employees. It was assumed that coaching was a sort of behavior modification technique used to correct a problem, similar to how computers could multiply numbers or process documents.

Then coaching was found to enhance performance of executive teams and build better leadership development processes that led to transforming capabilities to a broader part of the organization. Now, coaching is used to transform cultures and build the core competencies of change throughout organizations.

Finally, organizations are finding that coaching services with a focus on marketplace objectives can enhance existing revenue-generating products and services. Coaching can speed product adoption, improve customer loyalty, and create new revenue sources.

USING COACHING TO CREATE WORKPLACES THAT THRIVE IN CHANGE

Coaching creates cultures and mindsets that embrace and thrive with change. Currently, coaching can play an active role in addressing two significant trends that impact organizational effectiveness. They are:

1. The speed of change

2. Changing expectations employees have of their organizations

Much has been written about the speed of change and the impact of technology in accelerating change. This environment is labeled as VUCA: variable, uncertain, complex, and ambiguous. These factors create a dynamic and uncertain environment that requires creative approaches to doing business and meeting change head-on with courage rather than fear. To prepare their workforce for needed agility and innovation, organizations are turning to coaching to integrate the core competencies of change into their culture. These new cultures powered by coaching integrate the key competencies of learning and mindset that power innovation and mitigate the fear of change.

In addition to the new VUCA world, we observe a second trend where employees are asking for much more from their organizations. The workplace has become a community that reflects "who I am." As we move from hometowns to urban centers, as we work longer hours, and as we see work integrate more and more into our personal lives, we are asking the workplace to be more of an expression of ourselves. In view of this trend, leaders are asking new kinds of questions. Some of these questions include:

- How should we treat one another?

- What values do we want to embed in our processes and products?

- Do we want our work community to enhance our humanity and foster a connection to emotions and values and the richness of what it means to be human?

Coaching can help leaders connect people to values and spur them to action. It creates a less fearful workplace that results in a more optimistic, values-driven environment for both leaders and employees.

We all seek to be connected and recognized within a community. What if that community fully supports our ability to be human and grow through trial and error? What if it enables us to connect on a profound level with our own nature? What if we continue to deepen our understanding of our emotional nature as well as that of our community? What if we can work together to create a community that honors diverse values and enhances our ability to motivate ourselves and each other?

USING COACHING STRATEGICALLY TO CATALYZE CHANGE

We know of many organizational change initiatives that start off optimistically but don't achieve the results they sought. There are all too often company mergers and acquisitions, leadership training programs, succession plans, and culture change initiatives that fail to deliver. The reason behind these failures often lies in failing to address the obstacles posed by the human elements of change. These shifts require more than an instruction manual or a directive from leadership.

This is where using coaching strategically can catalyze organizational outcomes. Coaching helps leaders manage through complex changes.

The following are a few situations where coaching can be used strategically to address the human challenges:

- An organization requires employees and leaders to adapt and learn skills that are not part of their previous experience or training.

- A change in the organization structure that evokes resistance.

- Newly hired leaders require new processes of communication and decision-making.

- The underlying values of the organization change.

- An industry transformation requires the people at every level to make changes in behaviors and become more agile and enterprise focused.

- Succession-planning and diversity initiatives that require the adoption of new mindsets and focused competency-building.

- A coaching culture of growth mindset and supportive feedback delivery is needed to adopt rigorous but helpful personnel review policies.

All of the above require generative learning to achieve change, which we'll explore in more depth in chapter 3.

USING COACHING STRATEGICALLY TO BUILD COMPETITIVE ADVANTAGES

Early adoption of coaching by organizations can create competitive market advantages just as the early adoption of technology created competitive market advantages in the early days of IT development. Organizations that use coaching to gain competitive advantages can, effectively, be leaders in their field, and even disruptors in their industries.

> **Organizations that use coaching to gain competitive advantages can, effectively, be leaders in their field, and even disruptors in their industries.**

Coaching can help establish a variety of competitive advantages. Here are three effective ways:

1. Build workforce core competencies of change

2. Develop compelling places that attract and retain talent

3. Create product superiority

In the following sections, I'll further define these competitive advantages and provide an example of each.

Competitive Advantage 1: Build Workforce Core Competencies of Change

Organizations have created "coaching cultures" as a way to lead their industry in innovation and to avoid obsolescence in quickly changing industries. This "coaching culture" is created by deploying diverse types, tools, and models of coaching (see chapters 7, 8, and 9) to embed innovative mindsets and to enhance the kind of leadership that creates change-friendly organizations. The basic competencies include:

- The Open Mind—the ability to adopt new information and ideas

- The Curious Mind—the ability to challenge assumptions and the status quo and ask powerful questions

- The Optimistic Mind—the ability to think in terms of possibility and overcome hopelessness

- The Self-Aware Mind—the ability to explore and understand the self to better manage one's choices and impact on others

- The Other-Aware Mind—the ability to understand others

- The Values-Driven Spirit—the ability to align with purpose consistent with one's values

THE OPEN MIND
The ability to adopt new information and ideas

THE CURIOUS MIND
The ability to challenge assumptions and the status quo and ask powerful questions

THE VALUES-DRIVEN SPIRIT
The ability to align with purpose consistent with one's values

CORE COMPETENCIES OF CHANGE

THE OTHER-AWARE MIND
The ability to understand others

THE OPTIMISTIC MIND
The ability to think in terms of possibility and overcome hopelessness

THE SELF-AWARE MIND
The ability to explore and understand the self to better manage one's choices and impact on others

Examples of organizations adopting a coaching culture for their survival can be found in two case illustrations in this book, one a technology company and the other a petrol company. For the technology company, product innovation created an existential crisis as new technologies were replacing their own products and services. For the petrol company, the move toward more eco-friendly energy sources required a major shift in their product and service portfolio. These companies realized they had two options: build core competencies of change and growth mindset or become obsolete. (Read the full details about the technology company in *An Organization-Target Coaching Program Model Example* on p. 190 and the petrol company in *A Company Applies a Strategic Coaching Program to Transform Its Business* on p. 219.)

In another case, a healthcare company embraced a coaching culture as the foundation to prepare for a fast-paced internal culture switch. The organization wanted to step away from its top-down leadership structure. To replace it, the company sought a servant-style leadership approach that encouraged collaboration. (Read the full details in *An Organization Changes Its Culture by Building Growth Mindsets* on p. 69.)

To establish a coaching culture, these organizations embedded diverse types, tools, and models of coaching, including coaching with senior executives and teams; large-scale coach offerings to employees using internal, external, and coach-scaling organizations; coach skills training; AI behavior modification; and peer and group coaching.

CASE ILLUSTRATION

SAP Catalyzes Culture Change with Coaching

When faced with the move to cloud technology, SAP realized they needed to change more than just the technology. The firm sought a workforce that was more flexible and adaptable to change. SAP also recognized their leaders and employees needed to build new skills to meet this shift.

In response, SAP strategically built a continuous learning culture to meet this challenge. Franziska Weis, Global Peer Learning Lead–Coaching and Mentoring for SAP, states that they now "build leaders to lead from the head and the heart and to help others grow by sparking their passion, encouraging them to think big, and fostering collaboration and connection across the organization."

SAP values self-awareness in their people. They also want self-reflection to be a part of their employees' journey of learning. When thinking about the culture they wanted to create, SAP opted to define and promote a list of specific behaviors they would like to see in their leaders.

In addition, the company defined the three key leadership behaviors called "How We Lead," which were developed through input from over two thousand employees. These are:

- Unlock potential
- Explore possibilities
- Make it happen together

Having clarity of culture and leadership behaviors guided the development of talent throughout their training, coaching, and mentoring programs. Today, SAP's coaching program provides coaches to any of its one hundred thousand employees upon request.

The program contains 650 part-time coaches, as well as access to external coaches for senior leaders.

To maintain a high-quality coaching program, the internal coaches receive ICF accredited training. To continue the development of their coaching skills, coach peer learning groups were created whereby coaches share learnings from ongoing training or conferences. These internal coaches may take up to 5 percent of their work time to coach.

In pairing the coach to client, the HR department recommends the employee select a coach who is not in their area. In this way biases of positional power or other forms of bias do not interfere.

SAP integrates coaching with their leadership training by providing their internal coaches with all the information from leadership training programs in the company. This ensures the coach and client are speaking the same language and are aware of the key competencies required of leaders at SAP. As additional trainings are developed as part of their "Upskilling Series," SAP ensures the new content is shared with the coaches.

The company quickly recognized the power of coaching skills to build growth mindsets that fit with their continuous learning culture. They integrated "Coachable Moments" training into their leadership development training programs and made this training available to all employees. These programs help employees build coaching mindsets with powerful questions, curiosity and inquiry, and empowerment. They assist in recognizing the "coaching moment" when a coaching conversation can be most powerfully applied.

SAP recently added team coaches to their coaching services portfolio. Franziska says, "Team coaching helps teams work together with others and within their wider environment. It creates lasting change by developing safe and trusting relationships, better ways of working, and new thinking so that teams maximize their collective potential, purpose, and performance goals."

SAP believes team coaching builds resilience and collaboration and assists in the move to greater self-leadership required in today's increasingly complex world.

As one of the world's leading producers of software for the management of business processes, SAP has a robust technology platform called **SuccessFactors**, which houses the mentoring and coaching program tools. On the site, employees can define their needs and have the system provide choices for training, coaching, mentoring, and other forms of support. The system assists employees to view the bios of the worldwide portfolio of coaches. When approvals are needed, HR can view the information and commit online approvals for the employee. Various tools and knowledge content are also in the system to dovetail with the coaching and other talent development tools.

Organizations that design and use strategic coaching programs include diverse types, tools, and models of coaching. By deploying coaching holistically, they build the desired innovative and generative learning culture. Throughout the book, you'll notice examples of organizations that have chosen to create a coaching culture to meet change more quickly and effectively.

Competitive Advantage 2: Develop Compelling Workplaces That Attract and Retain Talent

As talent becomes the driver for organizational success, there's a greater need to attract and retain both young and mature personnel. The younger generation desires development and feedback, and coaching can provide that tailored, ongoing support. As a result, coaching strongly appeals to individuals entering the workforce today. For mature leaders, coaching assists them in managing the stress created by the fast pace of change and the adjustments required in a changing workforce. When organizations use coaching strategically to address talent needs, they create a more inspiring and supportive environment that attracts and retains both young and mature leaders, thus giving the organization a competitive edge in the talent marketplace.

CASE ILLUSTRATION

A Company Gains a Competitive Advantage in the Talent Marketplace through Coaching

Nick Halder led the establishment of a coaching program at an 1,800-person technology company based in the United Kingdom. At first, his goal was to address his immediate concerns. These two concerns were:

1. How do we create talent that have an open mind in adopting a broader technical knowledge base than their specific knowledge area?

2. How can we catalyze our entry-level talent development, so they are productive more quickly?

Nick decided to develop an internal coaching program by training interested employees in the skills of coaching. These skills included the techniques of inquiry and growth mindset. For scientists trained in the binary thought process of right and wrong, this was a significant growth area. The coaches then committed two hours or more a week to coaching others in the organization. The initiatives led to ongoing coaching of 150 employees at a time.

The success of this application of coaching caused Nick to develop a people leader training program that offered training in coaching skills. The introductory module of this à la carte training program was a coach-led debrief of the employee's style and 360 assessments. (Learn more about 360 assessments in chapter 8.) The experience introduced many employees to the power of coaching and a growth mindset for professional development. This, in turn, led a majority of training participants to take the coaching skills classes.

Nick found that those who went through the coaching training were more adept at giving and receiving feedback, empowering others to problem solve, and building trusting team cultures. The results of these programs evolved the company culture to a growth mindset culture. Employees were far more open to change in themselves and to different opinions and ways of executing on goals. They had gained the ability to meet change with agility.

The benefits didn't stop there. The company received an award in the UK for being the top technology firm for their entry-level training programs. The award was based on surveys of employees that touted the company's investment in them and their professional growth. They attributed their advancement to the entry-level coaching approach.

With a competitive market for technology talent, this put Nick's company ahead of the marketplace. Nick says, "Coaching is the most significant game changer in being able to create an agile organization that can move quickly and evolve."

Competitive Advantage 3: Create Product Superiority

Coaching services, when used in tandem with existing products and services, provide a powerful tool to ensure product adoption and customer loyalty. For this reason, many change management firms and other types of consultancies are using coaching to enhance adoption and implementation of their research, analysis, and recommendation services. A myriad of other types of companies, such as software producers, communications firms, leadership training firms, and recruiting firms, are embedding coaching into existing and new products for product superiority in the marketplace.

CASE ILLUSTRATION

A Recruiting Company Uses Coaching to Gain Product Superiority

A recruiting firm realized that many organizations find it difficult to integrate new executives. After helping to find and place a new executive, the recruiting firm would often observe a pattern. The new executive would try to adopt new systems, build new relationships, and adjust to a new culture. All too often, the process would take too long. Disruption and misunderstanding would surround the new executive.

The recruiting firm was aware that senior executives are an expensive resource to any organization. They are the most highly compensated and are instrumental to an organization's success. When an organization loses a senior executive, the cost of their replacement is significant.

With these concerns in mind, the recruiting firm designed a new strategy. This approach would help new executives build the skills of emotional intelligence and generative learning, which in turn would enable them to more readily adapt to the organization's environment. Senior executives would be more likely to stay, which would be more cost-effective for the organization.

For the new strategy, the recruiting firm added coaching to its services. It offered to find new executives, negotiate and hire them, and then provide six months of integration coaching to ensure the hire's success. This add-on service gives a layer of protection for organizations. They can invest in the new executive with lower risk of confronting failure and replacement issues. In this way, the recruiting firm built a competitive advantage in the recruitment marketplace by offering a service to ensure new executive success and reduce potential costs of a failed hire.

COACHING AND SOCIETY

In addition to impacting an organization, coaching has the power to transform society. Today we live in a world full of existential threats, including environmental degradation, wealth imbalances, and inequitable access to resources and healthy livelihoods.

When we consider these problems, the issues can seem too big for one person to solve alone and creates a feeling of overwhelm. It can even produce a sense of negativity and lack of hope. The pessimistic mindset inhibits the ability to find solutions and stifles the energy needed to create change.

These global challenges don't have simple tactical fixes. Rather, they require adaptive change and generative learning. They call for us to overcome biases and collaborate together to find new solutions, fail, and then try again. We must learn to teach ourselves to learn together and realize a benefit for all as opposed to a few. We must have the core competencies to meet fear and move forward. All of these are human challenges, not technical fixes.

Often, pessimistic mindsets come from a place of fear. We might have a sense of fear that is based on our traditions, livelihoods, personal connections, locations, and values. It is common to be afraid of the unknown. Coaching is able to help us, as a society, examine those fears. It can create in society the ability to take major steps toward greater understanding of ourselves and others.

Imagine a world that is more open to growth and change. Morel Fourman, an International Coaching Federation Foundation board member, shared this wisdom. He said, "We need to find the leverage points to make a difference," and in these key leverage points is where we can apply core competencies of coaching, including powerful inquiry, building of choices, and uncovering possibilities through new mindsets. This focus is represented by the work of the ICF Foundation, which has created a program to link pro bono coaching to the UN's Sustainable Development Goals. I will share details of a project that deployed coaching and impacted eighty educational organizations and 410 education leaders in North and South America, Asia, Europe, and Middle and East Africa.

"Coaching is about how to be a better human."
—JANET HARVEY, FORMER PRESIDENT OF ICF GLOBAL

To fully grasp how coaching can be strategically applied to drive change and achieve organization goals, it's worth taking some time to see where coaching is at in today's world. In the following chapter, we'll explore how our understanding of coaching and its use has developed in recent years. We'll also consider how it can help connect people to their values and emotions.

CHAPTER SUMMARY: AT A GLANCE

- Today, people—and their ability to navigate change—are the most important resource that organizations have.

- The speed of change, coupled with employees' changing expectations, is driving the need for coaching in organizations.

- Coaching can be used to develop an organization that can more readily adapt to change, and to even thrive in change.

- Coaching has followed a path that is similar to technology; it has advanced from singular uses into a powerful tool that can be used to propel strategic organizational outcomes.

- Organizations are achieving competitive advantages in many ways through the use of coaching, including:

  ▫ Building workforce core competencies of change

  ▫ Developing compelling places that attract talent and retain

  ▫ Creating product superiority

- The benefits of coaching today can extend beyond an organization and reach entire societies around the globe.

CHAPTER 2

Emotions and Values in the Workplace

"Our feelings are not there to be cast out or conquered. They're there to be engaged and expressed with imagination and intelligence."

—T. K. COLEMAN, DIRECTOR OF ENTREPRENEURIAL EDUCATION FOR THE FOUNDATION FOR ECONOMIC EDUCATION

Consider the wide range of emotions you have experienced in the workplace. Remember the times you felt optimistic or even passionate about a project? Also, recall what it was like when you felt demotivated, disappointed, and even angry.

All these emotions are present in every moment of our lives, including the workplace. Values underlie our emotions. A value is something that we hold as important in our life. Values come into play in the choices we make. When we feel an action is in conflict with our values, we may resist or procrastinate. Recall, too, the times that you are energized by a sense of relevance and purpose stemming from an alignment of your values and the work you do. Interestingly, we often are not conscious of this connection between emotions, values, and action (or lack of action).

Recognizing the role of emotions and values in the workplace is central to a strong workforce. In this chapter, we'll consider how emotions, and particularly anxiety, impact our workplace environments. We'll also look at the role of values as a key factor in action and inaction.

EMOTIONS IN THE WORKPLACE

Being emotional and having emotions are two distinctly different things. When we experience our emotions yet refrain from fully expressing them in the moment or choose our words carefully to manage a difficult conversation, we are not devoid of emotions. Instead, we are *managing them for a desired outcome.* Though we may not be aware of it at any given moment, our underlying emotions are always present within us.

In every personal or professional situation, accepting our emotions and not judging them is a *crucial* first step to managing them.

In every personal or professional situation, accepting our emotions and not judging them is a *crucial* first step to managing them. Listening to them can give us the ability to make better decisions and have better conversations. Our emotions can give us insight into what lies under the surface of the presenting issues. We can consider their meaning and what our intuition is trying to tell us. By identifying and beginning to use those emotions wisely, we can access a level of deep, primal information that will help us to make the best decisions, have the best interactions, and arrive at optimal solutions.

We have all experienced those moments when our emotions overwhelm our ability to respond to others effectively. We may lash out or retreat, and the underlying issue remains unresolved. This biological reaction has its roots in our fears of perceived threats to our identity and values. When we experience fear or anxiety, we are unable to think clearly. The sense of fear is a part of the human condition. It's a filter that gives us time to assess a situation before moving forward and taking action.

Fear makes logical thinking more difficult.

Neuroscience informs us that, when faced with risk, we respond with anxiety or fear. Our brains react with fight, flight, or freeze. The fear and anxiety overpower our logical brain and inhibit our ability to respond logically.

When we feel fatigued, insecure, or under stress, we respond with fight, flight, or freeze more readily. We may become short-tempered or lash out when we perceive events are going against our best interests. Gnawing anxiety overwhelms logical decision-making. We default to self-protection strategies instead of strategies that benefit the whole team or community.

Fear and anxiety of various types and intensities are present in the workplace. I focus on fear as the emotion, as it relates most often to the diverse emotions that impact our ability to act. Fear can be viewed along a spectrum of emotion ranging from discomfort to anxiety and terror. Some of the basic drivers of fear include our sense of security, control, connection, and competence. Depending on the level of intensity, fear can manifest in different ways.

FEAR LEVELS AND HOW THEY MANIFEST

	HIGH INTENSITY: FEAR	MIDINTENSITY: ANXIETY	LOW INTENSITY: DISCOMFORT
Security	This reorganization implies my firing is imminent.	This reorganization could change my team composition and productivity.	I will need to build new relationships with this reorganization.
Control	I don't have control of my financial portfolio as the market crashes.	The market is changing fast. I don't have a clear idea of the right strategy.	I may not have the right answer, but I will give it a try.
Connection	When this news of my malfeasance breaks, I will lose my professional credibility.	When I am promoted above my colleagues, I won't have their same support and friendship.	I will give this critical feedback despite the possible negative reaction.
Competence	What did I do wrong? It isn't clear why I was passed over for promotion again and they are restructuring the job.	I don't know if my lack of computer savviness will mean my transfer to a new job.	I haven't led a large division before, but I will do my best.

When fear is pervasive in the workplace, our nervous systems become overwhelmed. To diminish this sense of fear in the workplace, we can put a strategy in place to manage it. This can be done through emotionally intelligent leaders who know how to apply coaching principles.

THE NEGATIVE EFFECTS OF NOT ADDRESSING EMOTIONS IN THE WORKPLACE

While emotions are part of our everyday lives, the culture of many workplaces is built on the premise that we act in a generally acceptable, "professional" manner at work. This "professional" term implies being unemotional. The environment downplays emotions and their impact on productivity.

To a certain degree, the premise is useful. It allows us to separate personal interests from the interests of the enterprise. We can look at problems from the point of view of the organization mission. We are also able to follow more formal communication patterns that strive for clarity, precision, and nonemotional content. There is an adherence to process that allows us to choose to adopt norms. These norms serve productivity and efficiency. They also include values such as collaboration and respect.

However, we can often feel alienated from ourselves when organizations ignore the emotional content of our work, or when an organization's values appear to be at odds with our own. This can lead to cynical behaviors and attitudes. These, in turn, can create low morale and increased resistance. A downturn in productivity often follows.

ORGANIZATIONAL CHANGE AND EMOTIONS

We like to think that when we meet a challenge, we bring the best part of ourselves to bear. However, we know all too well that we can shrink back into fear-based behaviors that often defeat our ability to lead confidently and intelligently.

Change of any kind in an organization can trigger a series of emotions that often go unmanaged or addressed in the workplace. In her groundbreaking work, Elisabeth Kübler-Ross studied how humans react to change. She identified four stages during the process:

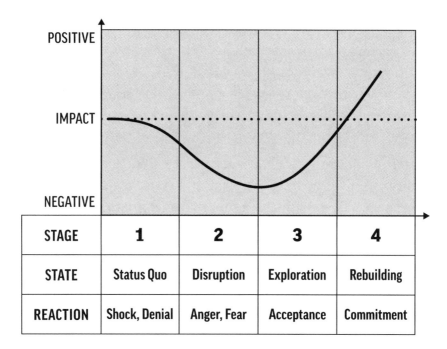

STAGE	1	2	3	4
STATE	Status Quo	Disruption	Exploration	Rebuilding
REACTION	Shock, Denial	Anger, Fear	Acceptance	Commitment

The human reaction to change according to Elisabeth Kübler-Ross.
Source: Scribner Publishing Group, from On Death and Dying *by Dr. Elisabeth Kübler-Ross. Copyright 1969 by Elisabeth Kübler-Ross; copyright renewed 1997 by Elisabeth Kübler-Ross. All rights reserved.*

Elisabeth Kübler-Ross's work on grief and loss provides a timeless model of human reaction to change. This model demonstrates that initially we respond with shock and denial when our status quo is disrupted. This can lead to anger and fear. Productivity drops as we are hijacked by our negative emotions.

Over time, we explore new possibilities in how to address change and move into acceptance. Productivity increases as we rebuild our approaches to doing business. We develop a commitment to the new methods. Note that the loss of productivity increases when the length of time required to move from stage 2 to stage 4 increases. This is where coaching can play a role in accelerating between stages.

"Discomfort is always a necessary part of enlightenment."
—PEARL CLEAGE, PLAYWRIGHT, ESSAYIST, NOVELIST, POET, AND POLITICAL ACTIVIST

CASE ILLUSTRATION

Human Reaction to a Change in Technology
An organization decided to bring in new technologies to improve its operations. Improvements would be realized throughout the company, including billing, HR management, sales tracking, and executive reporting. As the project rolled out, the leadership team proudly announced the implementation of a state-of-the-art IT change.

During the project, IT professionals collected data on how the systems operated. They crafted a technology system to replace human hours with faster and more efficient technology. They trained those who would use the technology. Finally, they launched the new technologies.

The result was a difficult process of push and pull between the IT department and the users. Pessimism and pushback set in. People said, "It takes more time than the old way. It doesn't solve problems—it creates problems." Fear of losing their jobs and loss of confidence in their own competence led to a drop in morale. Competition between departments increased as people sought to control more territory to prove their relevance and power.

The adoption process moved at a glacial rate. As a result, the organization went through lengthy stretches of reduced productivity and were not able to establish the full functionality of the system.

What creates the shock, denial, anger, and fear is different for each person. When facing a slow adoption of change, executives often resort to selling the change *harder*. They might explain all the benefits or even threaten the workforce with the dangers of not changing. The underlying barriers and emotional responses to change—shock, denial, anger, and fear—go unaddressed.

Since change is constant, we are continually put under stress. Negative reactions to change can lead to unproductive behaviors throughout the organization. Simply stated, change creates exhaustion. We need to make change less costly and incur less of a toll on our people.

"I can say that I like a challenge, and you tell me it's painless. You don't know what pain is."

—FROM "BITCH, DON'T KILL MY VIBE" BY KENDRICK LAMAR, RAPPER, SONGWRITER, RECORD PRODUCER, AND PULITZER PRIZE WINNER

VALUES IN THE WORKPLACE

Values are the principles or concepts that we hold as important. They are powerful forces below the surface of all our choices. Values guide our decisions of which family members and friends we choose to interact with, and where and how we choose to live.

Within our workplace, values guide our actions either consciously or unconsciously every day. When our values are aligned with our organization's goals and processes, we find work to be fulfilling and in flow. However, when our values are challenged in the workplace, decisions become harder. These moments can encompass a complex mix of competing values that slow down our ability to act.

> **When our values are aligned with our organization's goals and processes, we find work to be fulfilling and in flow.**

"Everybody's at war with different things … I'm at war with my own heart sometimes."

—TUPAC SHAKUR, RAPPER AND ACTOR

Identifying a values conflict can begin by evaluating our emotions. If we feel an emotion such as anxiety or anger, it could be a sign of competing values. We may go into "avoid" mode and not take any action without a conscious awareness.

CASE ILLUSTRATION

Recognizing and Overcoming Conflicting Values

A client was assigned the difficult task of telling a large group of employees that they would be let go. When we met to coach on this challenge, the client was anxious and unable to act. After some conversation to uncover the emotions around anxiety, he identified two key values that were in conflict. One was to "do the right thing for the enterprise." He believed in the need to fire the group so that the company could invest those resources in more promising lines of business. If the group remained, the company would continue to suffer losses that impeded its ability to support the other lines of business. However, in conflict with that value was his sense of loyalty and care for the people. He knew many of them and considered himself an empathic leader. How could he be an empathic leader and do the right thing for the enterprise?

Once we identified the two key values in conflict, the client was able to see that he could use empathy in how he approached the termination process. He cleared his calendar and spent significant time with each employee. He helped them to process the shock and pledged his assistance with helping them find new positions elsewhere. A severance package was arranged that included a career coach for the professionals, and he introduced the individuals to some key network contacts.

During the process, the leader increased his emotional intelligence by identifying his emotions in a more granular way that allowed him to see the values at play in this decision. This insight allowed him to find a creative solution and move more quickly into action.

Values also serve as the foundation for a sense of purpose and meaning in our lives. In my coaching, I find it essential for clients to rejuvenate their motivation through connection to purpose and values in order to energize their work. The key values can be found in the mission or purpose of the work content, or in the processes of the work. These might include growing and advancing their staff or knowing that they are providing for their family and playing a key role in their community. When my clients can connect with values and purpose, their energy and forward momentum increases.

"The purpose of life is a life with a purpose. So I'd rather die for a cause than live a life that is worthless."
—FROM "THE MARTYR" BY IMMORTAL TECHNIQUE,
HIP HOP RECORDING ARTIST AND ACTIVIST

COACHING TO MANAGE EMOTIONS AND VALUES

Just as fear and anxiety and value conflicts can lead to productivity losses, the opposite is also true. When we align values with emotions of excitement and enthusiasm, it can lead to high levels of productivity and creativity. If we can support our people through conflict, change, and other challenges that evoke fear or pessimism, we can unleash a much higher degree of productivity and job satisfaction. In doing so, we encourage an environment that is more receptive to change.

One of the greatest strengths of coaching is the ability to engage a client in a safe space where they can share emotions and turn them over and look at them. They can try to put words and thoughts to the emotions and ultimately use their own power to unlock more choices in their life and work.

What emotions might you need to understand in the workplace? The answer is simple: *in every situation where you find a decision, conversation, or relationship to be difficult.* This can include when you want to do something new, or you want to take a chance on innovation, creativity, or a new connection.

Think about those situations when they present themselves. Is there perhaps some hesitation, fear, excitement, or confusion? We often don't have the time or bandwidth to understand what is going on under the surface of these difficult situations. We tend to charge ahead into action without reflection. This approach may work some of the time, but what are we missing that could make these situations easy, effortless, or energizing instead of exhausting? By understanding and managing our emotions differently, we create the opportunity to achieve great results with an ease we didn't have before. The results of this approach are feelings of greater authenticity and presence—not faking it but rather being "in" it.

Coaching has a unique ability to catalyze the development of emotional intelligence. In addition, the teaching of coaching skills throughout an organization can create a culture of more human-centered leadership that supports the development of others.

A leader is able to build skills of emotional intelligence to be more deeply aware of their emotions. They are better able to manage their emotions toward the goals they seek. These leaders can learn to better read the emotions of others and then choose appropriate actions to drive better outcomes. These steps are defined as awareness and regulation of self and others:

	SELF	OTHERS
Awareness	Recognize feelings inside me and how they impact my behavior	Recognize others' emotions through empathy: • Feel the emotional temperature of the room
Regulation	Manage my emotions toward: • Optimism versus fatalism • Open mindset versus fear	Connect to emotions and others to influence them: • Engender inspiration • Assist with moving others to proactive action rather than reaction

Coaching is about unleashing the best part of humanity. It encompasses our ability to manage through overwhelming complexity, to be optimistic and hopeful, to seek to understand others, and to create and to solve problems. It provides a process for managing fear and insecurity, especially in the face of change. Coaching can also help identify and resolve value conflict. These efforts make it easier to navigate change, reduce feelings of pessimism, and increase productivity in the workplace.

We know that people are an organization's primary resource and that emotions and values are continually prevalent at the workplace; it's worth digging a little deeper into these connections. In the following chapter, we'll explore what I call the Human Challenge. We'll look at what the term means, why it's important, and how it relates to achieving organizational goals.

EARLY THOUGHT LEADERS IN
EMOTIONAL INTELLIGENCE

We now know that the strongest leaders are those that combine their intellectual abilities with strong emotional intelligence. Early pioneers Peter Salovey and John Mayer first defined "emotional intelligence" (EI) in 1990 as "... a set of skills hypothesized to contribute to the accurate appraisal and expression of emotion in oneself and in others, the effective regulation of emotion in self and others, and the use of feelings to motivate, plan, and achieve in one's life."[5]

Psychologist Daniel Goleman built off this concept. His book, *Emotional Intelligence*, popularized EI theory in the business world.[6] The book became the basis of assessments that measure EI and its impact on performance in the workplace.

CHAPTER SUMMARY: AT A GLANCE

- Emotions underlie how we act and react in all parts of our lives, including the workplace. By understanding emotions, we can manage them better.

- Change often engenders fear and anxiety. Fear in the workplace can be sourced to issues of security, control, connection, and competence.

- Values are what we hold to be important; when they are in conflict or not aligned in the workplace, it can be difficult to formulate actions forward.

- When we reconnect with the purpose or values underlying our work, we can achieve the feelings of passion and commitment.

- Coaching provides a unique opportunity for individuals to understand emotions and take action to manage them productively in the workplace. It also helps individuals understand how to articulate and align their values with work to create energy and forward momentum.

CHAPTER 3

The Human Challenge in Change

"I knew, even then, that whenever I nodded along in ignorance, I lost an opportunity, betrayed the wonder in me by privileging the appearance of knowing over the work of finding out."

—FROM *WE WERE EIGHT YEARS IN POWER: AN AMERICAN TRAGEDY* BY TA-NEHISI COATES, AUTHOR AND JOURNALIST

It may seem logical that a leader defines the goal and drives for the result through the implementation of new structures or systems. For simple technical challenges, this may suffice. For more complex change, addressing the Human Challenge will be required for success. As reference, the definition of the Human Challenge is listed at the beginning of this book, and also here:

WHAT IS THE "HUMAN CHALLENGE"?

The Human Challenge is our understanding and working with our sense of self and our human qualities. The Human Challenge is the effort to be able to recognize and articulate our own emotions, values, beliefs, and mindsets through introspective reflection and then use them to make choices rather than to engage in habitual response. When we articulate our emotions and values, we can uncover mental models and mindsets that we carry consciously and unconsciously. These mindsets, once seen, can be observed as choices rather than presumptions. Once we see that our mindset is a choice, it opens more alternatives in how we see ourselves and our limitations and opportunities. Importantly, the Human Challenge exists on an individual level, on a team or group level, an organization level, and even a societal level, as groups of individuals create mindsets and adopt beliefs that form the culture lens through which they collectively see the world.

In this chapter, we'll explore the importance of addressing the Human Challenge. We'll consider how it requires an adaptive process of generative learning rather than a technical fix. We'll also look at the benefits that come from instilling a growth mindset to address the Human Challenges in the workplace.

ADDRESSING THE HUMAN CHALLENGE AS A GENERATIVE LEARNING PROCESS

"Continuous improvement is better
than delayed perfection."
—MARK TWAIN, WRITER, HUMORIST, AND ENTREPRENEUR

Many leaders recognize that a change initiative requires strategic planning around the process. They develop communication plans and set up teams to assist the change. However, little is done to support the leaders and employees through the learning loop of complex change.

When we think about any change or initiative that an individual or organization undertakes, a coach asks, "What are the adaptive challenges versus the technical problems?" There are stark differences between the two, and it's critical to first clarify what each of these means.

A technical problem is one that requires a concrete answer. It generally has a clear solution. It can be overcome easily by seeking out the knowledge required. For example, a technical problem may be to determine how many people under the age of forty work in the company. The answer is concrete, and the means to determine the answer are straightforward. Once determined, there is no need to revisit the problem.

Changes that require a process of generative learning, applying the learning, and then repeating the cycle of trial and error to ultimately find a final solution are called adaptive challenges. They engage the Human Challenge of recognizing and articulating emotions, values, beliefs, and mindsets through introspective reflection. They then use them to make choices rather than to engage in habitual response.

The exact set of difficulties will depend on the situation, along with the culture, structure, and industry in which the organization operates. The following are some examples of changes that present a Human Challenge:

CHANGES	EXAMPLES
New structures	Change from matrix to hierarchy, centralized to decentralized; global versus domestic reporting; shift programs under administration
New systems	Change reporting lines, policies, and procedures; change financial reporting, sales reporting, or incentive systems
Culture	Hire a younger generation workforce; increase virtual work; go public; launch a strong diversity program
Business shifts	Mergers, acquisitions, large-scale layoffs, domestic to global leadership
New strategy	Increase technology use over manpower; shift market focus; shut down lines of production, distribution, or marketing
Skills shift	Require technology skills not previously used; require leadership skills in addition to technical skills

Unfortunately, in these types of changes, leaders sometimes approach the problem with questions that focus only on the process. They don't account for the people and the impact the change will have on them. Logically, they ask questions such as:

- What do we need to do?

- How long will it take?

- Who will lead?

At times, these questions may expand beyond process. They might account for issues related to competencies, behaviors, and knowledge needs. In these instances, the questions might include:

- What competencies will this require in our people?

- What behaviors do we need to see?

- What knowledge will they need to have?

The above questions still fail to dig into what may really get in the way of change. To fully understand the Human Challenge involved, a leader will ask the following questions:

- Who is impacted in this change?

- What fears may those impacted be required to navigate to make the change (e.g., a sense of competency, job, or other types of security loss; change in the ability to control or influence their environment; professional and personal relationship threats and loss)?

- What shifts in institutional or individual values is this change requiring?

- What mindsets will need to be different?

- What must we do to support our people through the trial and error of the learning loop in change?

During the COVID-19 pandemic, I observed leaders who failed to address the Human Challenges presented by the switch to virtual work. Some of my clients who reported to these leaders had young children who required supervised homeschooling during work hours or were responsible for the welfare of elderly, ailing parents. These unreflective leaders failed to ask what emotional support was needed for their people.

Faced with dilemmas when the Human Challenge wasn't addressed, a number of my clients were looking at leaving their organizations. Some were suffering from extreme stress that inhibited their ability to do their job. When sustained over time, this level of stress and resentment affected the employee, the morale of the organizations, and the ability to retain talent.

Luckily, I was able to coach individuals to self-advocate during this time. I also worked with leaders to help them understand the Human Challenge. Once they addressed the Human Challenge, many of the stresses of the change were eased for all involved.

CASE ILLUSTRATION

A Leader Understands the Importance of Addressing the Human Challenge during the Pandemic

A leader's workforce of seven thousand people moved to a virtual environment during the COVID-19 outbreak. The shift dramatically impacted the employees, and suddenly they found themselves at home, adjusting to a new workplace.

In addition to addressing the technical problems presented by remote work, this thoughtful leader took the time to ask, "What emotional impacts or values are at play in this change?"

After considering the answer, he took two powerful actions:

1. He incorporated one-on-one reach-out phone calls, making himself available to speak with people at all levels of the organization.

2. He held large-scale information meetings to address issues as they happened.

The one-on-one meetings came as a shock for some of the lower-level employees. They were surprised to pick up the phone and have such a high-level leader ask them, "How are you doing? What is hardest for you? What can we do to help?" While not all seven thousand employees could be included in this initiative, the word spread among employees that this leader understood the changes had real, human consequences—and he cared.

The second initiative of organization-wide meetings had the effect of potentially saving a life. The leader brought a panel of high-level experts to talk at an open virtual meeting. They spoke with the whole enterprise about the pandemic-related changes. One of the panelists was a high-level medical officer. The medical officer generously gave out his email to the two thousand participants in the virtual meeting and said, "If you feel isolated and are at risk, please reach out." During the meeting, a participant sent the medical officer an email stating they were imminently considering self-harm. The medical officer immediately departed the virtual meeting to provide support to the employee.

HUMAN CHALLENGES REQUIRE GENERATIVE LEARNING

In the book *The Practice of Adaptive Leadership: Tools and Tactics for Changing Your Organization and the World,* authors Heifetz, Grashow, and Linsky expand upon adaptive challenges.[7] They state their importance and give clear examples of how to learn generatively to overcome adaptive challenges. This generative process consists of the continuous experimentation of iterative steps. These include: trying an action, learning from it, making a change to suit the information gained in the first step, establishing new actions, and continuing through the process.

It's important for organizations to understand that most change involves adaptive challenges. Overcoming these requires generative learning. This is an ongoing engagement, rather than a specific end point.

The following example reveals the distinction between a technical problem and adaptive challenge and solution.

CASE ILLUSTRATION

A Pharmaceutical Company Faces an Adaptive Change Requiring Generative Learning

A pharmaceutical company hired only the best scientific talent. While this grounded their scientific expertise, they lacked the leadership skills to manage talent and provide strong leaders for their growing business.

As a result, the organization had gaps in their succession plan. To resolve these holes, the organization wanted to build young leaders earlier in their careers. Doing so would deepen the leader pool.

The first approach to solving the problem was technical in nature. The organization changed the internal review system with senior leader feedback to their reports from a system of twice per year tied to promotion and compensation to a just-in-time feedback system. In this new arrangement, leaders critiqued reports' performance more continuously.

Unfortunately, this strategy led to a high attrition rate. The senior leaders were delivering feedback that was perhaps in alignment with their scientific training, since their background in science was focused on technical accuracy and quality. When they encountered issues with their employees, however, they branded them in a manner that employees processed them as faulty or wrong.

They didn't, however, apply an understanding of the emotional intelligence skills needed to deliver the feedback effectively. Those receiving the critiques struggled to comprehend. Both leaders and reports lacked a mindset of growth.

The CEO realized that a simple technical solution, which had consisted of changing the personnel review system, was not enough to develop future leaders. They needed a culture change to move senior leadership mindsets from critical evaluation to supportive, coachlike feedback focused on growth of the junior leader rather than criticism. This was a generative change that required both training and coaching.

The CEO and HR department worked together to hire an outside coaching consultant. With the consultant, they designed a coaching solution that included both coaching skills training and coaching one-on-one for the executive team. The coaching skills training consisted of a two-day program, which taught coaching skills to roughly five hundred managers and executives, including the executive team. The training was interactive to help leaders understand the impact of inquiry and listening, and to help them create not just coaching skills but also a coaching and growth mindset.

Importantly, the twelve-member executive team was coached one-on-one for a year to ensure integration of both the coaching skills and the coaching mindset. It was essential for the executive team to most profoundly adopt a shift in values. They needed to think about feedback as a positive growth experience instead of an evaluation process.

The efforts led to a change in the executive team's mindset. They engaged in a learning loop of practice and had a positive result. Senior leaders coached junior leaders to build their ability to take on higher levels of management. The attrition numbers declined, and the leadership pool increased.

Generative learning is especially crucial in the development of leaders. Managing conflict, sharing leadership, listening, mentoring, and growing talent were cited as the competencies that were in most need of improvement, according to a survey by Stanford and the Miles Group.[8] These skills all require generative learning. The following graphic further depicts the survey's findings:

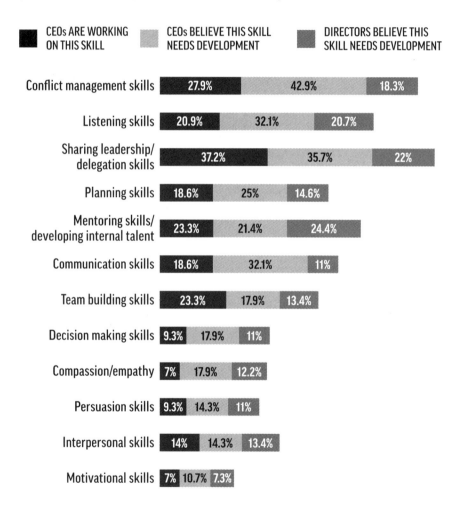

Source: 2013 Executive Coaching Survey, Stanford University and the Miles Group

Historically, building leadership competencies has been conducted through seminars and training, but much of the learning has been found not to be retained by the participants. German psychologist Hermann Ebbinghaus pioneered experimental studies of memory in the late nineteenth century. His research culminated with his discovery of the "forgetting curve." He found that if new information isn't applied into action, we'll forget about 75 percent of it after just six days.

Coaching provides a real-time experiential, reflection-based learning process that leads to far more learning. Imagine the difference between learning the theory of conflict management and then being asked to translate theory to action in a unique situation a month later. The brain struggles to convert theory to tactics and must also deal with the emotions that arise when dealing with a real conflict situation. Pairing coaching with training assists the client in the logical translations required from theory to tactics in a real situation and then helps uncover the emotional barriers and how to manage them. This creates an optimal environment for the client to learn.

> **Coaching provides a real-time experiential, reflection-based learning process that leads to far more learning.**

This holds true in organizations. When an organization is faced with change, it works best when there is a "learning loop" culture. The "learning loop" involves reflective time to assess what is not working, time to develop new actions, and the culture of support to experiment and be comfortable with it not being perfect. This allows the organization to integrate what works and develop strategies for what doesn't.

In his book *The Fifth Discipline*, Peter Senge championed "the learning organization."[9] He defined a learning organization as one that consciously builds awareness through developing feedback systems that collect data on how the organization is performing. The learning organization creates an environment where self-critique is viewed positively; therefore, learning can occur.

OVERCOMING THE HUMAN CHALLENGE OF FIXED MINDSET

Sometimes, I will meet a client who will draw a line in the sand about what is possible. They might point out a variant of the following:

"I am just not someone who …

… holds people accountable."

… is comfortable giving speeches."

… can hold a top leadership position."

… expresses my feelings at work."

… can deal with conflict."

… can stand up to authority."

Their statements ring true to many of us. We all have times when we compare ourselves to others. We do so in a way that precludes the possibility that we can achieve that admirable trait. We will say, "I can't be like them because I am an introvert." We might state, "I'm not smart enough" or "I don't have the right stuff," and so on.

All these statements are a reflection of a fixed mindset. We all have fixed beliefs in some parts of our lives. When we stay attached to them, they limit us in ways that are unimaginable.

How my clients perceive themselves, along with what might be possible, is contained in a small box with a tightly sealed lid. That limiting belief will shut down their ability to grow, change, or find new solutions to a problem. Coaching the fixed mindset and finding the possibility of growth is about liberation. This involves a liberation from fixed beliefs, which opens up a world of choices.

"Sit down before fact like a little child, and be prepared to give up every preconceived notion, follow humbly wherever and to whatever abyss Nature leads or you shall learn nothing."

—T. H. HUXLEY, BIOLOGIST AND ANTHROPOLOGIST

Carol S. Dweck addresses the challenge of adopting a growth mindset in her book, *Mindset: The Psychology of Success.*[10] She defines a growth mindset as the ability to see one's abilities as a starting point for growth and learning, rather than a fixed end point. Compare this to the typical fixed mindset, in which an individual believes they either have it or they don't. They perceive there is a single correct answer or solution. They will need to find the right one to succeed. In a fixed mindset model, there is a need to be right the first time, rather than engage in a learning process. The following graph further contrasts the differences between a fixed mindset and a growth mindset:

FIXED MINDSET		GROWTH MINDSET
I am wrong.	**Improvement and change**	I look forward to being better.
If I don't have what it takes, I never will.	**Confidence in ability**	I can learn the things I don't know.
I am bad.	**Critical feedback**	This shows me where to improve.
I don't like their success.	**Success of others**	I admire their success.

In this visual, we see the fixed mindset implies some of the following beliefs:

- Admitting there might be a better way to do something would imply that I am wrong (e.g., "If I agree that it would be better to do it your way, then I would be saying I am bad or failed").

- If it doesn't come naturally to me, then I can't do it (e.g., "I can't be a public speaker because I am bad at it").

- Receiving critical feedback demonstrates an unchangeable flaw (e.g., "When you say I am bad at listening, it means I will never listen well").

- I will never be as good as others at things I don't do well now (e.g., "My friend can be a salesperson, but I can't because I don't do it well now").

A fixed mindset limits both the potential of the organization's leaders and employees. It also reduces the ability of the organization to grow and change. Goals may be set, but it will be difficult—if not impossible—to achieve them if the Human Challenge is not addressed.

Given this, overcoming the Human Challenge of a fixed mindset is one of the biggest opportunities for an organization. It involves confronting the possibility that we won't necessarily get it right the first time. It also brings up feelings of vulnerability and challenges our sense of competence or security. Replacing fixed mindsets with growth mindsets calls for the processes of constructive feedback, experimentation, and integration to engender change.

"You may not control all the events that happen to you, but you can decide not to be reduced by them."
—FROM *LETTER TO MY DAUGHTER* BY MAYA ANGELOU, POET, MEMOIRIST, AND CIVIL RIGHTS ACTIVIST

CASE ILLUSTRATION

An Organization Changes Its Culture by Building Growth Mindsets

A large healthcare system had a history of leadership that created a culture of reactivity. Several hospital presidents had led with fear-based strategies. If their commands weren't followed, there could be reprisals. These might come in the form of public embarrassment, stunted career growth, and even firing. As a result, lower-level leaders simply waited for instructions from the top. A fixed mindset was embedded into the culture. In it, there was one right answer. Any experimentation that might not work was punished.

The healthcare organization brought on a new CEO who had a successful history of transforming a previous healthcare organization. The goal with the new leadership was to change from a command-and-control structure to an institution that valued leading through its people.

To get started, the CEO launched an organization-wide culture change. This new culture would have a "growth mindset." The ability of the senior leadership to adopt and carry out a growth mindset in their practices was assessed. Some members of the senior team were weeded out and replaced within a short time frame.

The CEO also established a new set of values and behavior expectations for his leadership. These included collaboration, respect and inclusiveness, and enterprise mindset. He set a powerful new structure in place, which consisted of a team leadership model at both the executive and hospital level. The model encouraged mutual decision-making and also supported holistic and creative problem-solving. Teams for the Chief Nursing Officer, the Chief Medical Officer, and the Head of Administration were formed at both the executive and hospital level.

At first, the collaborative decision-making was quite awkward. The old mindset of guarding against mistakes or being wrong was hard to break. Individuals at all levels faced a multitude of adaptive challenges.

To support their movement to a growth mindset, the CEO hired me as an outside Coaching Program Strategist (CPS). He wanted to align executive and senior team coaching to the new culture behaviors and values.

In the early days of culture change, there were numerous personnel changes and changes in reporting relationships. These required leaders to adapt to new personalities and styles, often more than once over the first year. I observed the following fears related to the old reactive culture and leadership style:

- *Insecurity*: Many asked, "Whom do I please to be sure I don't do anything wrong?" and "Who will have my back with the new leadership?"

- *Incompetency*: Personnel wondered, "How do I do my old job in a new way?"

- *Lack of control*: Oftentimes, leaders wondered, "Do I own this decision?" or "What if I lose my voice in the new system?"

The culture change called for constant adaptation each day to shed old habits and try new, unfamiliar processes. Every leader had to become more innovative and take on the challenge of trying new ways of doing things. The adaptive challenge of making decisions without full information or the certainty that they would succeed was especially hard for doctors trained to manage risk.

For some leaders, the greatest area of challenge was moving from a reactive mindset with "no mistakes allowed" to an innovative mindset of "let me try something and manage the risk." For others, it was how to form relationships with new individuals without the remnants of competitiveness that had plagued the former culture. Most leaders were challenged by managing through change, which required extraordinary effort to complete the job at hand and build the new organization. This involved longer hours and more stress.

To work through these challenges, the organization implemented a combination of individual and team coaching. The wise restructuring of teams, the power of clarity in values and expectations, and the coaching to work through the adaptive challenges paid off. The CEO achieved extraordinary change within a short amount of time.

In an organizational context, transformation is defined as a process of profound and radical change that orients an organization in a new direction and takes it to an entirely different level of operation or effectiveness. When coaching is used strategically, rather than tactically, it has the opportunity to assist with organizational transformation. In the following chapter, we'll look at how coaching can be used to address the Human Challenge and lead to both organization outcomes and transformation.

CHAPTER SUMMARY:
AT A GLANCE

- The Human Challenge consists of the emotions, values, and mindsets we bring to our existence.

- Organizations can catalyze their outcomes if they have an understanding and respect for the Human Challenge presented by change.

- Many of the challenges of the workplace are not fixed with technical solutions; rather, they require generative learning of trial and error.

- Learning new behaviors, competencies, and skills requires generative learning that benefits from the deep inquiry, support, and empowerment of coaching.

- Replacing fixed mindsets that won't allow for a learning process with growth mindsets that are open to trial and error and generative learning presents a significant opportunity for an organization to build the core competencies of change.

CHAPTER 4

Human Challenge Coaching: More Than Behavioral Change

"I did not know then that this is what life is—just when you master the geometry of one world, it slips away, and suddenly again, you're swarmed by strange shapes and impossible angles."

—FROM *THE BEAUTIFUL STRUGGLE: A FATHER, TWO SONS, AND AN UNLIKELY ROAD TO MANHOOD* BY TA-NEHISI COATES, AUTHOR AND JOURNALIST

To address the Human Challenge, coaching must reach deeply into the mindsets, values, and emotions of the client. We have many people in our lives that can assist us with problem-solving such as mentors, supervisors, and thought partners. While coaches use problem-solving-focused coaching, it is the Human Challenge coaching that achieves more transformative and lasting change for their clients.

The core competencies of change are realized in a growth and learning mindset. Human Challenge coaching can reach the emotions and values that help to engender the following competencies:

- The Open Mind—the ability to adopt new information and ideas

- The Curious Mind—the ability to challenge assumptions and the status quo and ask powerful questions

- The Optimistic Mind—the ability to think in terms of possibility and overcome hopelessness

- The Self-Aware Mind—the ability to explore and understand the self to better manage one's choices and impact on others

- The Other-Aware Mind—the ability to understand others

- The Values-Driven Spirit—the ability to align with purpose consistent with one's values

THE OPEN MIND
The ability to adopt new information and ideas

THE CURIOUS MIND
The ability to challenge assumptions and the status quo and ask powerful questions

THE VALUES-DRIVEN SPIRIT
The ability to align with purpose consistent with one's values

CORE COMPETENCIES OF CHANGE

THE OPTIMISTIC MIND
The ability to think in terms of possibility and overcome hopelessness

THE OTHER-AWARE MIND
The ability to understand others

THE SELF-AWARE MIND
The ability to explore and understand the self to better manage one's choices and impact on others

In this chapter, we'll consider how Human Challenge coaching can be used at an individual level, along with organization-wide endeavors. We'll see how Human Challenge coaching has a greater impact than mere behavioral changes. We'll also spend time comparing coaching to other techniques used to help individuals and organizations work through challenges.

HUMAN CHALLENGE COACHING TO CATALYZE INDIVIDUAL TRANSFORMATION

Individual transformation involves an individual shifting their mindsets or understanding in ways that affect more than just a single problem. It changes the way that client will assess and solve many problems across their professional and personal lives. Human Challenge coaching is about the person solving the problem, not the problem itself. It involves their mindsets, beliefs, assumptions, and values. If the person changes their mindset toward something or uncovers assumptions that they choose to revise or reject, the problem at hand will be impacted. Moreover, the many future situations that use these mindsets or understanding will also be impacted. This is why Human Challenge coaching focuses on the person solving the problem.

To see how Human Challenge coaching can be used to help transform individuals, we'll consider an example from one of my coaching clients. We'll follow his story, starting with the challenges he faced. We'll consider how the approach that I took with coaching, which involved a Human Challenge approach, helped him create a new mindset that was ready for the future.

USING HUMAN CHALLENGE COACHING: BEYOND THE PROMOTION

Don was the head of a high-performing group of research scientists. Three years prior, when he started leading the group, he found his leadership approach to be reactive. The group simply responded to requests from Sales and Marketing for new products and services. Nothing got developed unless it was asked for.

Don saw the opportunity to contribute more to the company. His group could proactively research areas of new product and services. They could attend industry conferences, network with industry colleagues, and collaborate with Marketing on research projects. By implementing these initiatives, Don's group was able to double the new product and services output. They played a more proactive role in the direction of the company.

Don was proud of his abilities. He felt he deserved a promotion and potentially the ability to oversee a second research team that needed the same strategy. He wanted to meet with his boss about the promotion. He delayed the meeting, however, as he wasn't sure how to go about it.

The Problem-Solving/Behavior Modification Approach

If I had addressed this situation in a nontransformative, problem-solving way, I would have articulated the problem as the conversation with the boss. We would have then created a framework for solving it. It may have been helpful but not as powerful.

The process might have started with me saying, "Let's write down all the value you bring to the company that reflects a higher-level position and would make you deserving of a promotion. Then, let's talk about how you might approach your boss in the conversation. We'll go over tone, wording, how to make the ask … and let's also talk about what objections might come up so you are prepared."

While this could be a fruitful way to accomplish a singular objective, I knew Don was looking for more. I also recognized his company would benefit from him overcoming the Human Challenges involved.

The Human Challenge-Centered Approach

This method, which is the one I chose, doesn't jump at the immediate problem, which in Don's case was the conversation with his boss. Instead, it asks, "What about having this conversation is hard for you?"

In the first approach, we are assuming Don doesn't have the skills or has just not thought about how to approach the conversation. We could be wrong on both counts. By asking what is hard for Don, we are asking him to identify the issue here that has him stuck.

When I asked Don this second question, he responded, "I know I add a lot of value to the company, but I am worried about a couple things. I am not the kind of guy to brag about myself. It seems egotistical."

In his answers, Don was demonstrating the value of humbleness. This was an interesting area to explore with Don. I asked him about the value of humble and what it meant to him. As we dug into the definition, we realized there was a new perspective around asking for a promotion by stating your value.

Don said, "It really is a marketplace at play inside the company. My colleague is constantly talking about his value, and I keep quiet. He seems to get a lot of attention. I think I would be creating a fairer marketplace based on merit than on who bragged the loudest if I would be clear about what accomplishments and competencies my team and I bring to the company."

Don found a perspective where his actions weren't just acceptable; they were also in alignment with his marketplace values. Once he was comfortable with how to approach the value he brings with his boss, he found there was something else in the way of this conversation. "I hate conflict," he said. "I know what my boss is going to do when I bring this up. He is very confrontational—not in a mean way, but because he likes to present counter arguments of decisions. I really hate conflict and want to run the other way."

Now we had a new, very rich area for Don to consider, which was the ability to deal with situations that felt conflictual to him. Through exploring the feelings that came up for Don when he thought about engaging with his boss, he saw that conflict was closely associated with an all-or-nothing/win-lose mental model. Some past associations with conflict with people in power when he was younger led him to approach later relationships with this model.

I asked, "When do you have other situations when you engage with conflict?" Don brought up problem-solving with his team. They would discuss different solutions and take opposing sides to suss out the options. In fact, the kind of rigorous challenges he deployed to test scientific hypotheses with colleagues was a very comfortable place for him. He named this mental model the "Challenge to a Better Solution" model.

I asked him if he could go into the meeting with his boss with this new challenge model instead of the win-lose model. He said, "That's easy, because I actually believe that is the case with my boss. He is just challenging me for the best resolution to the problem."

Don now felt ready and prepared for the conversation. He was ready for future conversations and challenges. By working with mental models, values, and the feelings of discomfort, we were able to help Don get to the nexus of what was hard and solve it. The new mindset was both transformative and sustainable.

HOW HUMAN CHALLENGE COACHING IS TRANSFORMATIVE

Continuing with Don's story, let's consider a bit more how Human Challenge coaching covers more than just behavior changes. In the following charts, you'll see how a Human Challenge approach digs deeper into the problem and helps provide a long-term solution. Notice the true and sustainable transformation that comes from coaching with the Human Challenge in mind.

NON Transformative Problem-Solving/Behavior Change

PROBLEM

Don doesn't know how to have a conversation with his boss about a promotion.

COACH ASSUMES THE ISSUE IS DEFINING THE PROCESS

Coach provides framework to have the conversation.

PROBLEM-SOLVING

Tactics laid out: Create a script to the boss, build reasons that you are justified for the promotion, think about possible ways to counteract reservations.

RESULT

Don has the conversation and "muscles" through any concerns or discomfort.

Transformative Change and Problem-Solving

PROBLEM

I don't know how to have a conversation with my boss about a promotion.

COACH EXPLORES WHAT IS HARD FOR THE CLIENT

Client articulates concern about appearing to brag and fear of conflict.

COACHING THE PERSON

Exploration of the assumptions and mental models around bragging.
Exploration of the definition and beliefs around conflict.

COACHING THE PERSON

Don reframes his role at work as a member of a marketplace that
requires him to present his and his team's accomplishments.
This has long-term impact going forward for all future negotiations
and visibility efforts for Don and his team.

Don reframes "conflict" conversations as "challenge for the best answer"
conversations. This is a familiar approach Don never thought to use
when it came to conversations with people in power. It essentially
dissolves his concerns for this conversation and future conversations
with this boss and potentially other people in power.

RESULT

Don has the conversation with confidence.

SUSTAINABLE CHANGE

Don has a new frame on his value in the marketplace that makes
advocating for himself and his team not just acceptable but important.
Don uses perspective of healthy challenge to replace conflict as the
frame for rigorous conversations. He is no longer reluctant to have
conversations of all kinds with his boss.

HUMAN CHALLENGE COACHING VERSUS OTHER PROBLEM-SOLVING TECHNIQUES

Coaching is a formal approach that is distinctly different from other support approaches. Its greatest benefit lies in the ability to catalyze growth in individuals and teams to think and work better over the long term, rather than just solve problems in the short term. Coaching is used to support growth and change in well-performing individuals and teams, as opposed to historical uses such as to counsel people out of the organization or address problem employees who are on their way out. Coaching should be implemented to support organizational strategic goals.

Coaches may play multiple support roles. They might be consultants, therapists, or mentors. It is essential (and ethically responsible per the International Coaching Federation ethics code) to make the distinction of when one is operating as a coach or another professional. (In chapter 10, the challenges of internal coaches are more fully explored.) Organizations use terms such as peer coaching or mentoring that are not formal coaching, but rather potentially use the application of coaching skills. It is important to distinguish between using coaching skills and entering into a coaching relationship.

There are a number of other modalities that are different from coaching. These can be complemented by coaching and coaching skills. They include consulting and advising, mentoring, and therapy. In the following sections, we'll compare and contrast these different forms to coaching.

USING COACHING SKILLS VERSUS COACHING

There is an important distinction to be made between using coaching skills and coaching. Using coaching skills is the use of any number of coaching skills, such as deep listening and inquiry, without a formal coaching relationship. Many organizations are training their leaders and mentors to use coaching skills in the workplace. This benefits their employees and makes better leaders and mentors. They can learn to ask more powerful questions and listen for values and mindsets rather than just listen for the purpose of problem-solving.

Using coaching skills enhances the probability of the leader or mentor to empower the employee to solve problems.

Using coaching skills enhances the probability of the leader or mentor to empower the employee to solve problems. It may not achieve the same level of transformation in the employee due to trust interference from positional power or competing interests present in the workplace. It is also very challenging to hold back advice, strong bias, and opinions when you sit in the same work environment as the client.

Coaching, on the other hand, is a particular relationship set up between a coach and client that has a clear structure. The structure is both with the relationship as a whole, as well as within each coaching session. Thus, a coaching relationship includes a contracted relationship for a set time length or for a number of sessions in which the coach and client will work together. There will be goals to the coaching, co-established by the coach and client, and alignment with organizational goals where relevant. There will be a clear articulation about the norms of the relationship, including confidentiality, frequency of meetings, roles and responsibilities of the coach and client, and how coaching works as a generative process and not a consulting arrangement.

A contract is formed between coach and client that outlines these elements of the relationship. It spells out what the role of the coach will be, not just with the client but also with the sponsor or institution and leader who may be sponsoring the relationship. It is important to note that the coach is not held responsible for the outcomes of the client. The coach is the catalyst to help the client achieve results but cannot be held accountable for the outcomes. A sample coaching contract follows:

SAMPLE COACHING CONTRACT BETWEEN CLIENT AND COACH

Coaching Agreement

1. Coaching is a client-coach partnership to facilitate the development of the Client's personal, professional, or business goals and to plan and provide support for achieving those goals. It is a comprehensive process that may involve areas of life beyond work, business, or leadership issues and may touch on patterns impacting success in other areas including health, relationships, education, and recreation, as appropriately serves the Client.

2. The Client understands that the Coach's processes and program materials are proprietary information and agrees not to disclose or use said information for purposes or business without the permission of the Coach.

3. The Coach respects the Client's right to privacy. The Coach agrees to maintain verbal and written confidentiality of all Client information unless permission is received from the Client, except as required by law. The Coach will only break confidentiality if there is concern that the Client threatens harm to themselves or others. The Client agrees to have only name, contact information, and start and end dates of coaching shared with International Coaching Federation (ICF) staff members and/or other parties involved in the certification process for the sole purpose of verifying the

coaching relationship; no personal notes will be shared. According to the ethics of the coaching profession, topics may be anonymously and hypothetically shared with other coaching professionals for training, supervision, mentoring, and evaluation to further coach professional development and/or consultation purposes.

4. The Coach upholds ethical guidelines set forth by the ICF. The Client signature below indicates understanding of the nature of coaching as defined by the ICF and the Client's rights in alignment with the ICF philosophy and ethical standards of coaching as found at: https://coachfederation.org/code-of-ethics.

5. The Client assumes full responsibility for results and outcomes produced from the coaching relationship.

6. The Client understands that coaching is not a substitute for counseling, psychotherapy, psychoanalysis, mental health-care, or substance abuse treatment, and the Client will not use it in place of any form of diagnosis, treatment, or therapy.

7. The Client understands that coaching is not consulting. The Coach will not provide solutions, advice, counsel, or directive guidance; however, the Coach may offer ideas, options, suggestions, insights, observations, feedback, or strategies for the Client's consideration, and the Client always has ultimate responsibility for his or her choices, decisions, actions, plans, and behavior. The Client will seek independent professional guidance for legal, medical, financial, business, or other matters. The Client understands that all decisions in these areas are exclusively the Client's decisions and acknowledges that the Client's actions regarding them are the Client's sole responsibility.

8. The cancellation policy requires twenty-four-hour notice of cancellation, or the session will be charged. Termination of the coaching by either party will be conducted in writing with two weeks' notice.

In addition to a contract, each coaching session has a structure that ensures clarity of purpose, along with clear learnings and next steps. Within each session, the best practice is to establish a goal for the session, engage in thinking about the goal, and then reflect on the client takeaways and next steps.

The agenda for a coaching session might look like this:

Opening Discussion
- What would you like to talk about?
- What is hardest about that?
- What would you want to take away at the end of our session?
- Powerful questions based on the opening discussion

Reflection Time
- What are you taking away?
- What was most useful to you?
- How might these learnings impact the agenda/goal?

Next Steps
- What would you like to do with this learning?
- What might get in the way of these action steps?
- What support do you need to take these actions?

This structure demonstrates how coaching is a different kind of conversation from therapy, consulting, and often mentoring. To ensure powerful coaching that targets the key issue for the client, the coach uncovers what is *hard about this problem for the client*. Often, this is where the adaptive challenge sits.

For example, if the client states they want to figure out how to get a better job, a mentor or consultant or advisor will often jump into the process of the job search. This is the technical problem-solving mode. They might discuss questions like, "How do I search opportunities?" "To whom do I talk?" and "What time line do I want?"

The generative coaching model assumes the client is most likely capable of figuring out these technical aspects of the job search. A brief conversation about the how-to can identify what resources are available to help with the technical challenge. The coach then asks, "What is hard about this challenge for you?" Then, the client enters into the sphere of the Human Challenge that is most likely generative. The client may say something like:

- "I want to work part-time, but I will never get paid what I am worth" (an assumption to be explored).

- "I hate networking" (a fear-based aversion to be addressed).

- "I hate asking for more; I don't think that is appropriate" (a belief to be considered).

Coaching also supports a generative learning process by acting as a support and accountability mechanism for the client across sessions. The client enters the learning loop by strategizing actions in the next steps phase of the coaching, completing the actions in between sessions, and then reflecting and integrating learnings in order to develop the next actions.

In this generative problem-solving space, transformation can occur. The client can use the sessions to break down barriers related to self-concept and limiting assumptions and see that more is possible.

Consulting and Advising versus Coaching

The consulting or advising relationship is based on the premise that the "coach" has expertise in management, organizations, or other areas ranging from science to public speaking. In this relationship, information will be given to the client that enhances their organization or themselves.

Some consulting firms conduct research to analyze the organization or technical area. They provide recommendations based on their synthesis of the data. While the consultant might characterize the relationship as a partnership, it is not a partnership of equals when it comes to the final action. Ultimately, the consultant is rendering judgment in the form of a recommendation.

Many internal coaches are actually advisors using coaching skills. They may have special knowledge about the organization's policies, politics, or people that the client is seeking counsel on. These advisory sessions are often short-term and problem-solving focused. They do not constitute a coaching relationship.

In contrast, coaches are carefully trained to avoid judgment and advice-giving. Their job is to assist the client in their search for solutions. If the client doesn't have the necessary expertise to solve the issues that arise during the coaching, then the coach works with the client to create a plan to find that expertise. This fundamental difference is where much of the power of coaching derives. It is like the old adage: "Give a man a fish, and you feed him for a day; teach a man to fish, and you feed him for a

The act of coaching instills a sense of perspective, confidence, and empowerment for the client.

lifetime." The act of coaching instills a sense of perspective, confidence, and empowerment for the client.

Mentoring versus Coaching

While the coaching relationship is a partnership of equals, the mentoring relationship is generally considered a relationship of unequals with regard to knowledge, information, or both. The mentor generally has information or knowledge that the mentee seeks from the mentor. For example, the senior leader may mentor a manager to help them understand how to succeed and reach higher levels of leadership. The mentor is able to impart knowledge about the culture, politics, organization process, and/or content of the work. The mentor may suggest individuals with whom to network and make introductions for the manager. They may also advocate for the manager. These are not the primary attributes of a coach and, in fact, can interfere with the empowerment aspect of the coaching relationship.

Mentors may have quite a bit of bias in what the mentee should do. The coach, on the other hand, is not advocating for a specific outcome. The coach may work with a client to engage their thinking about how to succeed in an organization and even suggest ideas. This information, however, is not advice but rather reflections on possibilities with no attachment to being the right solution. The mentor can often share perspectives that are built on their personal experiences and aren't trained to draw out the experiences of the mentee. This leads to assumptions on the part of the mentor as to the unique perspectives and issues that the mentee is dealing with.

Confidentiality is encouraged in mentoring relationships but not guaranteed. This lack of confidentiality will impact what the mentee will share. It will also affect the ability of a mentor to inquire deeply into certain areas like values, beliefs, and emotions, which could lead to more sustainable change.

These important differences will influence how effective a mentor can be beyond the imparting of information. That said, if the mentor is trained in coaching skills, they can adopt some of these key attributes that will make their mentorship more powerful. When using these coaching skills in the workplace, mentors will need to be aware of when they shift from inquiry to advice-giving, when they want to tell the client the right answer, and when they assume their mentees' perspectives and values.

Mentors will also need to adopt strict confidentiality protocols that they can prove to the mentee. Even if the mentor doesn't share confidences, they will need to prove to the mentee that they won't share information in the future or allow future interactions to be colored by the special knowledge of the mentee.

Therapy versus Coaching

Therapy is defined as a "treatment" that addresses emotional concerns or mental health issues. It may be provided by a variety of trained professionals, including psychiatrists, psychologists, social workers, or licensed counselors. According to *Psychology Today*, therapy involves examining and gaining insight into life choices and difficulties faced by individuals, couples, or families.[11]

The therapist's expertise is to diagnose and treat or to engage in a curative process. Coaching does not diagnose and treat underlying conditions or claim to cure. Instead, it presumes a healthy client. It partners with the client to engage in self-discovery and awareness, as it serves the goals of the client. The partnership of coach and client presumes that the coach is not a health expert but rather a thinking partner. The coach may challenge the client's thinking but does not claim to be the authority.

Because the coach deals with emotions and deep thinking with values, people may think coaching is therapy. As we see in the very premise of this book, the presence of emotions does not make an issue in need of a curative process. Rather, emotions provide keys to what values or preconceived ideas are important to a client in a decision-making process. And emotions come from the more primal place in our brain. They provide wisdom about solving for what is hard about the problem for the client.

For example, suppose a leader wants to have a difficult conversation with a partner in their business about dissolving the business. The idea of entering into the conversation engenders many diverse emotions for the client. The coach can ask the client to experience these emotions in real time and then reflect on what is there. The client is able to address the difficulty of having the conversation at its root cause. This is not a curative process but rather an exploratory and self-awareness process that allows the client to get into action.

In my training of coaches for an ACTP (Association for the Coaching and Tutoring Profession) accredited program called "Leadership Coaching for Organizational Performance," I see therapists, mentors, leaders, and educators. They go through the program to learn the skills of coaching. They use these competencies to enhance their own areas of expertise. In this sense, there has been a trend toward greater creativity in seeing what coaching can offer. The ways to deploy it have increased as well.

While it's worthwhile to see how coaching compares to other behavior-related techniques, it's also true that a true transformation typically requires Human Challenge coaching. We've seen an overview of it; in the following chapter, we'll explore what's needed to carry out Human Challenge coaching.

CHAPTER SUMMARY:
AT A GLANCE

- Coaching the Human Challenge is more than problem-solving; rather, it addresses the person solving the problem. When a client is coached, their ability to solve problems of any kind is enhanced, and therefore coaching creates sustainable change and empowers self-awareness and a growth mindset.

- Other support modalities are distinct from coaching:

  - Using coaching skills is an unstructured application of skills rather than a coaching process. It can be beneficial in building cultures with the core competencies of change.

  - Consulting and advisory services focus on advice-based engagement, while coaching takes an approach that aims to build on the client's ability to learn to solve for challenges.

  - Mentoring is a relationship where the mentor provides guidance as opposed to coaching where the partnership is among equals.

  - Therapy is a curative and diagnostic process, while coaching assumes a healthy client. Both modalities assist the client through self-discovery and awareness to build the muscle of self-management.

- Coaching is complementary to other modalities. Today, many leaders, therapists, mentors, and consultants are learning coaching skills to enhance their work.

CHAPTER 5

The Seven Competencies of Human Challenge Coaching

"Until you make the unconscious conscious, it will direct your life and you will call it fate."
—C. G. JUNG, PSYCHIATRIST AND PSYCHOANALYST

For coaches to coach the Human Challenge, I have found there are seven competencies a coach should be able to master. The competencies enable the coach to help the client achieve self-awareness and build new strategies for learning and change. These competencies can transform the client's leadership and their organizations.

Ultimately, using these competencies helps the client to unleash their human potential. The main competencies included in Human Challenge coaching to release the human potential are as follows:

1 Uncover and overcome emotion-based barriers

2 Change mindset and perspective

3 Build ownership and uncover assumptions

4 Reconnect to values that create motivation and drive

5 Enhance respect and understanding of other people

6 Integrate learning

7 Build confidence

When used in powerful coaching contexts, these competencies have the ability to create transformation. They delve into key areas related to emotions, values, and learning. They focus on coaching the person rather than the problem. In the following sections, we'll further observe these seven competencies.

1 UNCOVER AND OVERCOME EMOTION-BASED BARRIERS

Even the best and the brightest performers experience fear and discomfort in their workplace (as discussed in chapter 2). These emotions are often evoked when a leader faces the need to change. Deeply set fears can inhibit the leader from effectively executing the desired outcome.

The emotions may surface when the individual feels a direct threat that is related to one of their key drivers (see the chart in chapter 2: Fear Levels and How They Manifest). For instance, they may be struggling to have a sense of competence with a job change. They could feel their independence or ability to be in control is being threatened. Or they may fear a loss of a sense of belonging with a restructuring that isolates them from colleagues. They could even fear the loss of a job.

> "For it's our grief that gives us our gratitude,
> Shows us how to find hope, if we ever lose it.
> So ensure that this ache wasn't endured in vain:
> Do not ignore the pain. Give it purpose. Use it."
> —FROM "THE MIRACLE OF MORNING" BY
> AMANDA GORMAN, POET AND ACTIVIST

To undergo change, it's essential to help the client understand and work with their emotions and triggers. These include being aware of their emotional makeup and the intellectual patterns that they carry into any moment. This process requires looking below surface issues to the person behind the challenge. Think of it like working on a computer. In the coaching, we are working with the CPU, or brain, of the computer. We are not dealing with the software that is running on top of the computer.

CASE ILLUSTRATION

Helping a Client Overcome Emotion-Based Barriers

Dashell was a technical expert inside a professional services firm. The company faced increased market competition and needed to significantly lift their revenue growth targets. To help meet these goals, the firm asked Dashell to bring in new business.

His new duties consisted of selling more to current clients and bringing in new clients. In addition to this, he was asked to continue with his normal workload. To work through the change, Dashell came to me for coaching.

During our conversations, Dashell shared with me that, previously, his success in his job had always been based on his technical knowledge. Now, however, he would be judged on sales volume. The switch made him very uncomfortable. He expressed anger at the institution for "changing the rules of the game." He explained, "I studied and worked hard to be the best technical expert. Now, they want me to be a salesman!"

As we moved into the anger, he unearthed that he was, in fact, afraid to display incompetence. He felt he didn't have what it took to develop skills of relationship building and making the "ask." He thought he would do these tasks poorly. Furthermore, he felt a threat to his independence and ability to control the scope of his job. His resentment toward the firm at his loss of control was a huge barrier in wanting to adopt new skills.

As Dashell named the fears behind the change, he realized there were next steps he could take to address them. Through our coaching, he identified three next steps. They were to:

1. Network with a number of consultants that were known to be good salespeople. He would ask them how to develop the needed skills.

2. Attend client meetings with these consultants to watch them in action.

3. Receive coaching on mindsets on the topic of control, so he could regain a sense of mastery and ownership of his job.

In addition to this direct form of conversation to identify fears, coaching for emotions can use a technique called embodiment or somatic experience. The method helps the client be present with a whole-body experience of what comes up when they are faced with a challenge they want to overcome. The activity allows the client to become more aware of why they operate the way they do.

They can use the technique to uncover barriers to change. By becoming aware of the present state of the body, such as the heart rate or the clenching that comes with different moments in time, they gain greater understanding of themselves and the body and mind that approaches the problems in front of them.

In coaching, if we understand that present state, we may be able to name the emotions and thought patterns that are either helping or getting in the way of how we are tackling a problem. Once we're aware of these obstacles, we can set a path that leads to a positive solution. We know that when we approach a problem with optimism and vision, we release chemicals in our brain that are different than the chemicals released when we are fearfully running from a problem.

CASE ILLUSTRATION

Asking a Client to Try an Embodiment Approach

Diane and Jane started as friends and colleagues. Then Diane received a promotion and became Jane's boss. Over the course of the following year, Diane noticed significant changes in her relationship with Jane.

To begin, Diane observed that Jane's performance was lagging. At the same time, Diane found it increasingly difficult to address the issue and give Jane feedback. Jane started spreading negative gossip about the new direction of the organization under Diane. After a year of being Jane's boss, Diane came to me for coaching.

I asked Diane to try an embodiment approach to help her sort out the issues. She was initially skeptical but agreed to the exercise. I told her to become present with an imagined future moment when she would approach Jane to have a conversation.

This visualization helped Diane to experience the emotions and thoughts that were present for her in the relationship. I asked her to stay with the emotions that arose by noticing where she felt them and what they felt like in her body. Diane shared that she felt betrayal and deep disappointment. With further exploration, Diane realized the betrayal was rooted in her strong sense of loyalty as a friend. Diane told me, "If you are a friend, then you support someone beyond your self-interest and you advocate for each other. Jane breached that trust."

Once Diane identified this strong belief and recognized that Jane didn't share it, she felt a release from the strong emotional reaction to Jane. Diane said, "It is funny, but talking through the situation in this way—where I was in the emotional state—helped me to see what was underneath it and then release it."

Even though she had been unsure of the embodiment technique,

Diane was thrilled to discover its ability to uncover the root causes of an issue. By releasing her emotional holds on the situation, she increased her ability to act and move forward in a new way.

SELF-EXPLORATION EXERCISE

Think of a time when you were asked to change an aspect of your personal or professional life that was not of your own making, and it created an emotional reaction. Ask yourself, "Which of the following identity threats made the change hard?" It may have been one or more of the following:

- Competence
- Belonging
- Independence/control
- Security

Then ask yourself, "If I wanted to overcome that threat, what would I do?"

2 CHANGE MINDSET AND PERSPECTIVE

"The single story creates stereotypes, and the problem with stereotypes is not that they are untrue, but that they are incomplete. They make one story become the only story."

—CHIMAMANDA NGOZI ADICHIE, WRITER

We discussed overcoming the challenge of fixed mindset in chapter 3. The growth mindset is to see problems as challenges with optimism rather than pessimism. It is to take errors as an opportunity to improve rather than as a final assessment of what you can achieve.

There are many mindsets people can hold about a situation that describe their approach to a problem, and with coaching we use the identification of the current perspective and the application of a new perspective to unlock the client's choices.

If we think about mindset as a perspective, we will see how we can shift a mindset to see new possibilities. A perspective is similar to how you might approach looking through the lens of a camera. For instance, consider the following criteria that is addressed when snapping a scene of your family during a ski trip to the mountains:

- Do you take a wide angle shot so you can see the mountains behind your family?

- Do you zoom in on the faces of your family and make them the primary subject of the photograph?

- Do you photograph them as they ski down the mountain with the intention of recording their form on the slopes?

Each of these choices represents a perspective. What we often fail to recognize is that every moment is a choice in perspective. We can apply this concept of choosing a perspective to a workplace setting.

For instance, reflect on how you arrive at work. Do you enter the door with a sense of dread? If so, what might be behind the dread? Perhaps you feel resentment toward your leadership. Maybe they never show appreciation for all your effort. Therefore, the work seems burdensome. We might call this the "dread" perspective.

Continuing with this scenario, you may not feel that you can change leadership's ability to laud your work. You could, however, change the way you think about it. A new perspective might be to reset your thinking to the following: "I believe the difference I make is reflected in how I lead my team." Notice how this switches your focus to the value you bring to your team rather than the dread stemming from leadership's lack of recognition.

Trying on different perspectives also helps us open our access to new possible solutions. I once coached a consultant who was struggling to say "no" to work from a client. The client, however, was overly demanding. The consultant knew logically that she would be fine with turning down the work, but she couldn't muster the courage to say "no." In this case, I told her to name the perspective that she was in with the client. To do this, I asked her to "feel" what came up when confronted with the possibility of saying "no." She identified that perspective as "never enough." She felt a fear of financial insecurity. I then asked her to think of other places in her life and how she embodied them. One of the places she mentioned was running. She shared that she felt in control of her world when she moved in this way. She felt comfortable in her body and could choose where she ran and how fast she ran. She called this the "free" perspective. I had her "embody" that perspective and its feelings. Then I asked, "If you approach a conversation with the client from that perspective, what would occur?" Immediately, she knew how to have the conversation from a feeling of control rather than insecurity. The power of perspective comes from the shift from one embodied perspective to another.

The power of perspective comes from the shift from one embodied perspective to another.

"If you don't like something, change it. If you can't change it, change your attitude."
—MAYA ANGELOU

CASE ILLUSTRATION

Enabling a Client to Change Perspective

Anna was a leader in a policy research organization. When Joe, the program director, retired, Anna was promoted into the program leadership to take his place. Suddenly, she had to adopt a new perspective on her sense of self as leader.

As Anna prepared for her first town hall meeting with the staff and making the rounds of major funders, she found it difficult to see herself at that stage of leadership for several reasons. First, Joe had been a command-and-control type of leader. He had persuaded with his charisma. Anna, on the other hand, had always practiced collaborative leadership of her teams. Her perspective was that to follow Joe, she needed to take on those commanding qualities. Trying that style of leadership made her feel inauthentic and fearful that she couldn't replicate it effectively, as she had never practiced it. Second, Joe had built a reputation as a thought leader over decades in their field of research. Anna was in her early forties and still building her brand external to the organization. How could she seem credible to her funders? Her perspective was that only thought leaders could own the kind of gravitas that funders expected.

In our coaching, we first tackled the preparation for the town hall. Anna shared that when she imagined herself in her successor's shoes, she saw herself at the podium looking down on her employees with that distant commanding presence. She would be speaking to her audience and entertaining them with a Joe-like charisma that she felt was not true to her. Joe's presence was so cemented in her mind that she was unable to imagine anything different.

To unstick her "command-and-control perspective," I asked her to play with a visualization. Could she imagine herself in front of the town hall? Would she be behind the podium? Would she be on stage? Would she be "telling and promoting" or "sharing and asking"?

She quickly found a visualization that felt authentic. She saw herself sitting on a stool, not standing behind a podium. She would give an introduction of her heartfelt excitement for the program's future. She would share her vision and then ask the employees to ask questions or share their sense of the vision.

This visualization of her interactive and authentic self soon became a reality when the day of the town hall meeting arrived. By using her visualized approach, Anna received enthusiastic support from her employees. They embraced her authenticity and collaborative presence.

We then tackled the limiting perspective with the funders that, without being seen as the seasoned thought leader like Joe, she lacked the gravitas her funders expected. I asked her to imagine different perspectives of herself in relationship to her funders. She came up with "highly qualified researcher," the "strong networker," and the "grassroots mover and shaker." These were different aspects of herself that provided a context in which to show up with the funders. They were not Joe's "established thought leader" persona but rather aspects of herself that she could own.

After exploring each of the options, Anna settled on the combination of all three. She placed an emphasis on the "grassroots mover and shaker" that had established on-the-ground results from the policy research. This new perspective gave Anna confidence that she had all the gravitas she needed to stand in front of funders.

SELF-EXPLORATION EXERCISE

1. Think of a difficult conversation you need to have with someone. What feelings and thoughts come up? Name that perspective. For example, you might name the perspective "frustrated with their incompetence."

2. Now think of another relationship or situation that carries different feelings and thoughts. Name that perspective. Embody the perspective by raising memories of it in your mind. This perspective might be "looking forward to connecting."

3. As you think about how to approach the difficult conversation with the first person, you might find yourself back in your first perspective. Following our example, this would be "frustrated perspective." Replace that with the second "looking forward to connecting" perspective.

4. Ask yourself, "Coming from this perspective, how do I see it? How might the conversation go differently? What new thoughts arise about the relationship or situation?"

3 BUILD OWNERSHIP AND REPLACE ASSUMPTIONS

Ownership means that we accept the circumstances we have, recognize the issues they present, and make the choice to be the driver of the solution. Simple to say, but hard to execute. Seeing the situation as it truly is may be clouded by our assumptions of what is true or what we control. We often make assumptions that aren't accurate or applicable to the current situation. By identifying these assumptions, we can replace them with new assumptions more applicable to the situation.

For example, a client shared with me that, in their new position, "playing politics" got in the way of efficiency. The client was therefore ignoring her peers' concerns about her direction in order to push through the tasks that needed to get done. Through interviews I uncovered that her peers were not inclined to help her execute because she was too pushy and failed to address what they perceived to be major issues with her direction. In our coaching the client identified two faulty assumptions behind her current approach. The first was that efficiency in her current role was more important than "politics" or getting buy-in for her direction, when in fact it was slowing down achieving her goals. The second assumption was that politics is "bad." This negative assumption led her to avoid the conversations she needed to have.

CASE ILLUSTRATION

Helping a Client to Build Ownership

Michael was awarded a big job driving a new collaborative partnership for his company. The company was in the process of partnering with other financial institutions to create a new product line. This partnership and product line had huge revenue and prestige potential for the firm. Michael's leadership saw his driving, creative, problem-solving, and charismatic personality as the perfect fit to make this opportunity happen.

Michael dove into the challenge. True to form, he developed creative solutions and powerful relationships that progressed the initiative to the edge of success. However, as the final agreements for the partnership were being negotiated, he became increasingly frustrated with his leadership. He saw them as slow and plodding. They didn't seem to understand the new partnership and the import of what it could bring to the company. They kept dragging their feet on the final agreements.

In our coaching, Michael shared his concerns with me. He said, "Bureaucracy was one of the reasons this company may be the wrong one for me. After all, I am an entrepreneur." He thought he would wait until leadership figured it out.

To make matters worse, conflicts broke out within Michael's team. They started fighting over who would benefit from the future revenues and who might get credit for parts of the work generated by the initiative. This seemed petty and absurd to Michael. In our coaching, he asked, "Why can't they just do the hard work and see where the chips fall like I have? I've been working eighty-hour weeks to make this happen without looking for more compensation or recognition." Again, he stepped back from the challenge and decided to let the warring parties duke it out.

In the coaching, I challenged Michael on both fronts. What did he own in leadership's slow pace? What did he own about the in-fighting on his team? What beliefs was he carrying that were in his way to resolving these barriers?

I observed his blanket characterization of the leadership as "the bureaucracy." What did that mean to him? Yes, there were multiple layers of approvals required, but these were people who apparently didn't have enough understanding of the complex new initiative. What role did he play in that?

Michael confessed that, as a fairly young leader, he assumed senior leaders should understand the complex partnership arrangement. He didn't feel he had the right to navigate the leadership reluctance. He thought he should wait for them to come around.

Michael also realized his passivity in owning his team's conflicts. He identified his self-effacing value that it was unimportant to claim recognition and reward. He assumed this value should apply to everyone.

In our coaching, Michael realized these assumptions didn't have to stand. He developed a plan to educate and sell in the new initiative. He selected leaders who were most prone to move forward. Then, he organized a series of group meetings with the key stakeholder leaders. During those, he sought consensus to move forward.

As for his team in conflict, Michael understood that recognition and reward of a different kind were required for others. Once he saw this, he was able to take action. He dealt more directly in conflict resolution.

When Michael implemented his ownership of the leadership and team issues, the contracting process was catalyzed. His leadership noted his more proactive stance on both fronts. They rewarded him with praise and recognition of his growth as a leader.

SELF-EXPLORATION EXERCISE

Where in your life have you ceded responsibility or ownership? Where have you decided that "it's someone else's job to fix that"? Or perhaps, "I shouldn't have to be the one to ... ?"

Write a sentence that describes this situation.

Then jot down three reasons that the opposite is true—that you actually do have responsibility or control.

For example, you may write: "I should not bother building that relationship because they are more senior and should reach out to me." Now, what are three reasons why the opposite is true? You might pen, "I should reach out to them because they are more senior to me." Or "It shows my confidence. It shows I care about the people I work for. It demonstrates my initiative."

 RECONNECT TO VALUES THAT CREATE MOTIVATION AND DRIVE

"When I dare to be powerful, to use my strength in the service of my vision, then it becomes less and less important whether I am afraid."

—AUDRE LORDE, WRITER, FEMINIST, WOMANIST, LIBRARIAN, AND CIVIL RIGHTS ACTIVIST

Values can play a big role when we face making choices. This can be true even for simple decisions such as who should run a meeting. You might decide the key value to base the choice on is ensuring the right outcome is achieved in the meeting. Thus, as leader, you should run the meeting. Or you might have read a book on empowering others and struggle with the concept of letting your deputy take more control of the meeting. This trade-off of values is constantly present in our choices every day.

Often, we may struggle with decisions because we are not able to determine the values that are important and will help us make a decision. We may be in a confused state between two choices because we don't know what is important in the decision. Or we may procrastinate in our decision-making because we find that there are two important values in conflict. For example, I value both the ability to empower others as well as the ability to get the right outcome.

When this happens, issues related to a lack of motivation or slow decision-making can arise. We might get stuck and feel unable to take action. We can't seem to decide on the right direction, we procrastinate and flip-flop, or we get confused.

When working with values, the first step is to articulate what the values are that are at play in a situation. We need to articulate at a granular level what that value means to us. Values are subjective and uniquely defined. If I say "family" is an important value to me, what I mean by that will not necessarily be what someone else means. One person may believe it is to understand their heritage and honor their ancestors. Another may say family means responsibility for caretaking. A third person might state that family holds a central importance in their life as interpreted by their religion. Once the values embedded in the decision are clarified, we can more effectively weigh them in the situation at hand.

CASE ILLUSTRATION

Helping a Client Evaluate Values and Solve Conflicts

Alexandra was a top leader in a thriving corporation. The company targeted her as a future executive. As such, she was assigned coaching.

When she came to me, Alexandra had recently been promoted. This change meant she had to commute from Chicago to New York City each week to oversee her new team of product development engineers, sales and marketing managers, and product managers. She had built her previous team over several years. Her relationships with her people and customers had been one of the biggest rewards of her job.

As we started the coaching, I conducted 360 interviews with Alexandra's new reports, peers, and leaders. (Learn more about 360 interviews in chapter 8.) The findings indicated that while she was well viewed, people felt a lack of leadership from her. Alexandra didn't make herself available to them, and she didn't seem focused on the current business, despite an energized team of professionals around her.

At first, Alexandra balked at receiving the feedback. She protested that team engagement was, in fact, one of her leadership strengths. Surely that wasn't a development area for her!

As we coached together, it became clear that Alexandra held strong values of developing and supporting her people and building a culture of team first. However, she had failed to do that in her new position. She was feeling a lack of motivation to connect with her team despite her values.

Through further exploration, Alexandra shared she was struggling with the challenges presented to her family when she started commuting each week. The conflict between her sense of obligation to her family and her obligations to her team seemed irreconcilable. As a result, she had found herself not doing a good job of either.

Once it became clear what values were in conflict, Alexandra was able to work through some changes to her calendar and focus. She planned to work from home every Friday, so she could spend those evenings with her family rather than commuting. She worked from her Chicago office on Mondays. Then she spent the intervening days in New York.

With the new arrangement, Alexandra felt she could focus on the team building at work without feeling conflicted about her family. This ability allowed her to once again enjoy the work. She also realized she could be more attentive with her family when she was with them.

SELF-EXPLORATION EXERCISE

Where in your life do you feel stuck in taking action? Are you trying to resolve a difficult relationship? Choosing a different lifestyle? Deciding on a career path choice?

Think about the challenge. Then write down the values at play for you.

Now ask yourself, "Is there a way to maintain the values that are important to me and also take action?"

For example, perhaps you need to have a difficult conversation with a report about their performance. You have stalled, and yet the situation causes a great deal of frustration. What value is underlying that? Is it that you don't want to hurt their feelings? Is it that you feel you will come across as unlikeable? Or do you want to maintain harmony? By writing down the values that are important to you, you may be able to identify one that would be supportive of the conversation.

5 ENHANCE RESPECT AND UNDERSTANDING OF OTHER PEOPLE

Leaders profess again and again that the hardest part of the job is the people. They explain this statement by pointing to experiences they've had. They might mention demanding supervisors, competitive peers, and argumentative reports.

When we are frustrated with other people, we often blame them for the problem. If they were less or more of something, then we could get things done. But we can't necessarily change other people.

We can, however, change our understanding of them. We can find new ways to navigate their styles, needs, and foibles. Coaching supports leaders in understanding different styles and perspectives. It allows leaders to explore what might be possible in the relationship. This requires self-understanding. Leaders must ask themselves questions such as:

- What is important to me?

- What is my style?

- How am I perceived by others?

- How might I show up differently, given others' priorities and style?

CASE ILLUSTRATION

Team Members Grow in Appreciation for Each Other

A team came to me for some optimization coaching. They were doing "fine" as a team, they stated. However, there seemed to be some stress in the way work got done. Team members were finding themselves frustrated with each other and at times working at cross purposes.

I knew that teams are a rich arena for testing respect and understanding of others' communication and work styles. For the coaching, I conducted initial interviews with all the team members about what were the perceived strengths and weaknesses of the team. This revealed the following themes:

1. The team had too much to do with new assignments every week.

2. There was a low level of understanding of the priorities.

3. The rest of the organization seemed to think of the team's division as customer service representatives rather than a key engine of the operations of the organization.

The team facilitation started with a work style and motivations assessment completed by each member of the team. Debriefing the assessment as a group led to a sense of appreciation for the differences in style. What the team learned was that they were by nature strong, people-focused individuals. As one team member explained it, "I get the most energy from my work when I am helping others." As this was a team of support functions, the findings made sense.

Still, the team lacked strong system-builder styles. These are people who enjoy building processes for what needs to get done. In fact, the leader of the team was a high "creative" who thrived on new ways of doing things and taking on new projects, even if interest was lost after some time. The team came to understand that they lacked good systems for assessing projects and priorities.

Given this, the team decided to hire a project manager to track priorities and project progress at each meeting. The leader recognized his tendency to take on too many new initiatives and asked a member of the team who was more analytical to discuss how to integrate new projects into the ongoing calendar. Finally, the team recognized that while many of them liked the "support function" brand of supporting other parts of the organization, they needed to elevate their status as a group. They decided to brand their work to other parts of the organization as a "partnership." After all, without operations the work of the organization couldn't be achieved.

The next steps involved filling these identified gaps in team competencies. After our sessions, team members grew to appreciate each other's strengths. As a result, the team started to thrive.

SELF-EXPLORATION EXERCISE

Think of someone to whom you consider it is hard to relate. Perhaps this is someone who seems to approach problems from a really different perspective than you. What is it that is different about that person? What do you experience when you share the outcome of the issue you may be solving together (frustration, excitement, etc.)?

Now, put yourself in their shoes and think about a problem you would like to solve. Do you come up with a different answer than you would normally? Does it add richness to your perspective? Can you find what is good in that other perspective?

"You know, some people say life is short and that you could get hit by a bus at any moment and that you have to live each day like it's your last. Bullshit. Life is long. You're probably not gonna get hit by a bus. And you're gonna have to live with the choices you make for the next fifty years."

—CHRIS ROCK, COMEDIAN, ACTOR, WRITER, PRODUCER, AND DIRECTOR

6 INTEGRATE LEARNING

Making change is an adaptive problem that requires generative learning. When we use a learning loop, we can move through change and prepare for future changes. That's because the learning loop functions in the way its name implies. It allows us to become aware of the needed change, to articulate the real issue, to formulate actions, to process and reflect upon the results of the actions, and then to integrate learnings and create new next steps. If we think about where the loop breaks down in the workplace, we can potentially point to all these areas.

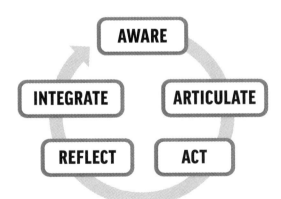

Adapted from Kolb, D. A. Experiential Learning: Experience as the Source of Learning and Development, *vol. 1. Englewood Cliffs, NJ: Prentice-Hall, 1984.*

Let's further define each of these areas to see how the learning loop plays out.

Aware: Becoming aware of an area of needed change can be hard. We often become aware when a change is imposed on us, and we know we must address it. Coaches support self-awareness through conducting assessments and interviews for the client.

Articulate: Some changes are so fraught with interfering thoughts, beliefs, and concerns that we first need to define what is really at issue with this problem. This is where the coach and client articulate what they are trying to solve for.

Act: We need to build possible actions to arrive at potential solutions, but without taking the time or finding a good thought partner we may find it too exhausting to even approach the brainstorming required. Often, people are stuck in old assumptions that close off creative brainstorming. Coaching gives support in this process.

Reflect: Once actions are taken, we need to analyze what went well and what went poorly. This requires the time and energy to be self-critical. Reflection is often shoved to the side in a fast-paced work world. Coaching provides a safe space to examine where we failed and where we succeeded in order to integrate the success and reboot the failures. Often in reflection, the real learning takes place. In the fast-paced nature of work where we focus on action day in and day out, reflection is rare.

Integrate: If we can navigate all these steps, then we can arrive at integration. This consists of building practices and habits that incorporate the new behaviors. The coach and client relationship tracks the learning and next steps from previous sessions. It can ensure that changes have formed into habits that require little thought. If there is something that isn't working, a new awareness is achieved, and the learning loop can restart.

Coaching is the tool that provides the time, space, and support to think analytically, articulate what is true, and build actions.

> **Coaching is the tool that provides the time, space, and support to think analytically, articulate what is true, and build actions.**

SELF-EXPLORATION EXERCISE

Think about the last talent or competency you tried to master. Then answer these questions:

- What created the awareness that you wanted to master the talent?
- How did you generate actions to master it?
- What time did you spend in reflecting on the results?
- What more could you have integrated from that experience?

7 BUILD CONFIDENCE

The coaching process serves as a form of empowerment through inquiry. It allows for a safe space to express fears and doubts and then to find solutions. Once the client experiences the unearthing and mastery of fears, they are far stronger and more confident that fear is surmountable. They know how to take the process of understanding and overcoming fear into the next challenge.

Coaching ultimately brings the client greater awareness about who they are. It affirms their ability to make choices and act from an authentic place. Clients understand and articulate their values and what creates meaning for them both personally and professionally. This "centering" gives them confidence in their capacity to make good choices and decisions.

Understanding others and building respect for different styles also translates to understanding and respect for oneself. Clients recognize that what they don't do well or are not interested in doing is not a deficiency. Rather, it is an opportunity to create solutions by building systems and partnerships.

"Everybody's somebody's everything. I know you right. Nobody's nothing. That's right."
—FROM "EVERYBODY'S SOMETHING" BY CHANCE THE RAPPER, RAPPER, SINGER, SONGWRITER, RECORD PRODUCER, ACTIVIST, ACTOR, AND PHILANTHROPIST

Finally, coaching can be used to build a greater capacity to learn and adapt. Essentially, it is a form of learning how to learn as an adult. Once clients understand they have the capacity to move from a fixed mindset to a growth mindset and can engage in the learning loop, the change is truly transformative. This process helps to increase confidence, as clients feel better prepared to face both current and future changes.

SELF-EXPLORATION EXERCISE

Think of a situation in which you feel less confident. Now ask yourself:

- What about this situation creates my lack of confidence?
- What gets in the way of tackling it rather than avoiding it?
- What do I need to learn to be confident in this situation?

We've spent some time defining the competencies needed for Human Challenge coaching. Addressing emotions, fears, and values allows us to create change that goes beyond a mere behavioral shift. Implementing the competencies can help create a change that ultimately supports other outcomes and builds competitive advantage. This, in turn, can help individuals release their human potential, which can take both them and their organization to new heights.

CHAPTER SUMMARY: AT A GLANCE

- *Human Challenge* coaching to unleash human potential requires seven competencies: uncover and overcome emotion-based barriers; change mindset and perspective; build ownership by replacing assumptions; reconnect to values that create motivation and drive; enhance respect and understanding of other people; integrate learning; and build confidence.

- Uncovering and overcoming emotion-based barriers help individuals grow in their awareness of their emotional makeup and response system.

- Coaching for emotions often utilizes embodiment, which allows a client to be present with a whole-body experience of a challenge they want to overcome.

- Changing mindset and perspective enables clients to try out different perspectives in order to build choices and find new possible solutions.

- Building ownership involves optimism, which helps clients believe a positive outcome is possible.

- Identifying underlying assumptions can open up new possibilities in problem-solving that are in the way of possible solutions.

- Reconnecting to values consists of articulating the values present in our choices, defining them, and then applying them when making a decision.

- Enhancing respect and understanding of other people helps leaders to both better comprehend themselves and appreciate others.

- To integrate learning, we go through a learning loop. A learning loop consists of becoming aware of the needed change, articulating the real issue, formulating actions, processing and reflecting on the results, and then integrating learnings and creating next steps.

- Building confidence happens when coaching provides a safe space for clients to explore situations, carry out inquiries about themselves and their challenges, and grow in their capability to learn. The process ultimately empowers clients to overcome current and future challenges.

Coaching in Organizations: The Seven Factors for Effective Coaching in Organizations

---

"A goal is just a dream with a deadline."

—DRAKE, RAPPER, SINGER, SONGWRITER, ACTOR, AND PRODUCER

Coaching in organizations requires special attention to areas of aligning to organizational goals, ownership of outcomes, and confidentiality, as well as attention to client ownership of the outcomes. For the coach it requires competencies in an enterprise view, inquiry absent of bias that includes bias toward the organization and a comfort with emotions in the workplace. By ensuring that these factors are in place, the coaching engagement will have more power and align more effectively with the goals of the organization. These factors are:

1 Clarity of organizational and/or leader coaching goals

2 Ownership of the coaching outcomes understood

3 Confidentiality and autonomy of the coaching process

4 Coach focus on client-generated solutions for client growth

5 Coach enterprise view

6 Coach inquiry absent of bias

7 Coach comfort with emotions in the workplace

In this chapter, we'll further define each of these factors. We'll see the part they each hold in achieving organizational outcomes through coaching. When they are all in place, the potential for change and competitive advantage is high.

CLARITY OF ORGANIZATIONAL AND/OR LEADER COACHING GOALS

If the organization has goals for the coaching, it's important that they are made clear to the coach or coaches, the sponsor, and the coaching client or clients. This step should be carried out prior to the beginning of the coaching. These goals should be revisited throughout the coaching process.

In my observations, there are often unclear messages to the client during the introduction phase. For instance, a leader might receive an email from an HR representative or their boss announcing the leader has been selected for coaching. The leader has no idea why they have been chosen.

During my first meeting with a client, they all too often confess to me that they are confused about the purpose of the coaching. Sometimes, they are worried they'll be fired. They think they've been selected because of a problem with their performance.

Having clear coaching goals for the coaching is vital. There are goals that the organization will have, as well as individual goals the client sets. These goals may continue to develop as the engagement goes forward. If the organization or sponsor has not clearly thought through and communicated the outcomes they hope to achieve from the coaching engagement, it is hard for the client to succeed in achieving these outcomes. Furthermore, those organizational goals need to be made clear to the client relative to their behavior. In other words, what will the client be doing differently as a result of the coaching? Chapter 9 outlines the process of creating goals and gives examples of how to translate these goals into the desired behaviors.

When I meet with a sponsor who tells me that they want their client to improve in a certain area, my first question is, "How has that been communicated to the client?" It is not the job of the coach to own the role of the client's leader. Rather, it is important that the coach play a role in assisting the sponsor and client in better articulating the outcomes desired by the sponsor. The section on alignment meetings (see chapter 8, "Alignment Meetings") outlines a process for this in detail.

When beginning the coaching, I recommend giving the potential client an opportunity to "opt in" to the coaching. The coaching sponsor can have a conversation with the client before the coaching begins. During this discussion, the sponsor can explain the organizational or leader expectations attached to the coaching. The potential client has a chance to ask questions, understand what is expected, and "opt in" to the process. When this is done, the coaching generally launches much more quickly and effectively.

The following chart is an example of a leadership development plan. It integrates organizational and client goals and encourages reflection on the goals' relevance to the organization.

CLIENT GOALS	CLIENT SUCCESS	CLIENT CHALLENGES	ORGANIZATION IMPACT
Managing up • Regularly share division success • Highlight team	I will feel comfortable sharing success, and leaders will have insight to top performers.	I dislike selling myself.	The division and I will have more visibility, providing more and better opportunities. The team will feel recognized by leaders.
Life balance is in a better place.	I will be able to focus on my family when I am at home.	I feel pulled in too many directions, and the stress is impacting my focus.	I will be more focused at work.
ORGANIZATION GOALS	**ORGANIZATION SUCCESS**	**CLIENT CHALLENGES**	**ORGANIZATION IMPACT**
The leader believes the tech team doesn't collaborate with the Sales department.	My team will have a reputation for working well with Sales: • Information dissemination • Client call teams	I don't understand what specifically the leader wants. I think the Sales department is difficult.	If we could collaborate with Sales, I think revenue would be impacted significantly.
Build selling skills.	Bring in $1 million of new business this year.	I took sales training, but I don't know how to apply it.	$1 million in new sales.

OWNERSHIP OF THE COACHING OUTCOMES UNDERSTOOD

The coaching contract with the organization is crucial in defining the role of the coach versus the role of the client. (See a sample coaching contract section in chapter 4.) Essentially, the client is responsible for the results or outcomes of the coaching. It is the coach's role to support them to achieve the outcomes.

The coach may participate in conversations with the sponsor during the precoaching process to understand what the needs of the sponsor are and how best to design the coaching engagement. In this way, the coach can help the organization sponsor gain clarity about the coaching goals.

Once the coaching begins, however, communication with the sponsor and coach about the coaching always includes the client. In general, the client drives the communication. This is because coaches don't make clients do things. Nor are they in a position to require them to do things. If that were the case, then coaching wouldn't be effective. It is the trusting partnership between coach and client that allows and empowers the client to unearth the barriers in the way of doing what they know the sponsor wants or what the client wants. In this partnership, the client can explore the best way to align their values and behaviors to the sponsor's requests. In some cases, this may lead to the client expressing disagreement with the goals they have been given.

> It is the trusting partnership between coach and client that allows and empowers the client to unearth the barriers in the way of doing what they know the sponsor wants or what the client wants.

If the client finds that the requested goal from the sponsor is unacceptable, the coach can support them in the communication with the sponsor to find alternative agreements. With most of my client engagements, there are life balance issues that get in the way of the work performance that they and their sponsor want to achieve. To even consider committing to the sponsor's expectations may require the client to build greater resilience or energy to engage in the learning process to adopt new ways. These are the places in which the coaching can engage.

3 CONFIDENTIALITY AND AUTONOMY OF THE COACHING PROCESS

Human Challenge coaching conversations often explore underlying values and emotions that drive the client's behavior. Doing so can help address the core of the issue rather than just the problem and solution of the moment. In this space, there are often deeply held convictions and values. Speaking about what is important is often emotional.

Sometimes these conversations strike a chord with clients right away. In one case, I came to a first meeting with a client. We started exploring where some of his strong values of leadership originated. He began talking about his early childhood and young adult experiences related to leadership. As he recalled these life-shaping events and moments that had helped him develop his skills, the executive became emotional. This was a conversation that was fundamental to his leadership, yet one he hadn't had in decades. The trusting and confidential process of coaching allowed him to visit these experiences in a safe space.

Throughout the coaching, the client must feel that the coach will hold the conversation confidential. The client also needs to know the coach will not reveal the coach's own impressions or opinions about the client to others. If the coaching is occurring with a team or multiple clients in an organization, it must be clear upfront what will be shared and what will not be shared. A best practice is typically that the coach wall off not just the conversations but also the coach's assessments about that person. Once a coach breaches or is perceived to breach confidentiality, trust plummets. Other potential clients will be reluctant to participate in coaching.

My work on the Independent Review Board (IRB) for the International Coaching Federation made the importance of confidentiality in coaching clear. The International Coaching Federation Ethics Code sets standards with confidentiality. (Read more about the ethics code at: coachingfederation.org/ethics/code-of-ethics.) The IRB reviews cases where breach of ethics may be present. To ensure good ethical practice, the coach and sponsor have a clear contract or agreement with how confidentiality will be handled. If the coach must share information with the supervisor or others in the organization, it must be clear what information is shared before the coaching engagement starts. Best practice for a trusting coaching relationship is that nothing in coaching conversations is shared, and the coach will not share opinions of the clients with others. For the internal coach, this can require careful contracting, so the client can protect themselves from the consequences of revealing more about themselves than they want, given the position of the internal coach. (I discuss the challenges to confidentiality for internal coaches in chapter 10.)

4 COACH FOCUS ON CLIENT-GENERATED SOLUTIONS FOR CLIENT GROWTH

A coach's job is to help the client think—not to think for them. A focus on client-generated solutions is one of the most distinguishing attributes of the Human Challenge coaching and differentiates it from other techniques like advising, consulting, and mentoring. (Chapter 4 further explains these differences.)

The purpose of the coaching is to enable the client to build more reflective and self-aware thinking skills and to create empowerment and confidence. To do this, the coach's job is to unearth what is hard for the client in solving a particular

A coach's job is to help the client think—not to think for them.

problem and help the client build skills and tools to navigate that or any problem. The coach will keep in mind that there is a key distinction between the problem and the person solving the problem. The question to ask is not "How should the client solve the problem?" Instead, the question is "Why is it hard for the client to solve this problem themselves?" Then, we move into that more generative space.

There will be many problems to solve for the client in their career. The coach's job is to help them be better at solving problems in general rather than solving the problem at hand. When we conduct Human Challenge coaching, we help clients dissect the barriers to the changes they seek rather than to maintain the status quo of reaction. This reflective process of inquiry helps them to build the ability to step back from a problem and see themselves and their reaction, and then to explore other ways of seeing the problem. This builds their ability to access creativity and possibility and leads to releasing their human potential.

In each coaching session, next steps are formulated in partnership with the client. Coaching is a partnership to get clients in action because it is through action that clients learn. Generative growth in the coach-client partnership is engaging the client in the learning loop to become aware of the needed change, to articulate what is really the issue, to formulate actions, to process and reflect upon the results of these actions, and then to integrate what works and recreate actions for what doesn't work.

"Coaching is unlocking people's potential to maximize their own performance. It is more often helping them to learn rather than teaching them."
—**JOHN WHITMORE, AUTHOR, COACH, AND RACING DRIVER**

There are four important elements of creating next steps in partnership with the client. They are:

- Reflection and synthesis

- Action identification

- Barrier exploration

- No-judgment "failures"

Before entering the next steps process at the end of the coaching session, it is crucial to ask the client, "What are you taking away from today's conversation?" The question moves the client's brain from exploration of the issue to synthesis of what they are now learning about the problem and about themselves. This can be a pivotal moment in the coaching conversation. In the answer, the client is accessing not just the problem itself but also their reactions to the problem. Once again, these may be their personal values, emotions, and so on.

If this question, or some form of it, is not present at the end of the session, then unconscious, deeper learning can be lost. These deeper learnings can be some of the most important origins of next steps. For example, at the end of one session, I asked a client to share their takeaway. They said, "I knew this bothered me, but I had no idea how angry this makes me. By seeing that, I think what is at stake is not just a job title change but rather a real breach of my integrity." With that revelation, the next steps were far different than what they would have been if this deeper connection had not been surfaced through the reflection question.

In order to create actions, coaches have built skills in brainstorming, planning, and gaining commitment. The coach always first asks what the client thinks are the best actions rather than jumping in with a coach solution question such as, "How about if you try this?" or "Wouldn't it be good if you tried that?" Those types of questions are really suggestions. Allowing the client to first do the thinking on next steps brings the client into empowerment rather than dependency on the coach. It helps the client shift from problem analysis and synthesis to their own "solution brain."

Often, clients express next steps as general, high-level actions. They might say, "I need to have a conversation with my direct report." Or they might state, "I need to start exercising." Those are actions, but they are far from clear. In fact, those statements may reflect the issue they came to the coaching with and not a novel action at all. In generating next steps, the coach might ask questions such as the following:

- What are the steps to that action?

- What support do you need to take that action?

- What might get in the way of that action?

- What do you need to remember to do that?

By answering these questions, the client gains specificity and clarity about the next steps. They might put reminders on their calendars. They also may feel a commitment about the next steps.

This ability to create actions is paired with a coach's nonjudgmental presence. The approach allows the client to return after trying the actions and discuss what didn't work, as well as what did work.

Failure or honoring the things that didn't work is important learning. It is all too often avoided because we don't like to admit to failure. And where the client does not take action, the coach provides a safe space to explore the environmental or personal barriers that got in the way of action. This exploration exercise can often reveal some of the unconscious fears or values the client has. By seeing them, the client can better navigate them moving forward.

5 COACH ENTERPRISE VIEW

Coaches who coach individuals and teams in organizations are better coaches when they recognize how organizations function and the implications of different organization cultures. This understanding can come from an academic background such as an MBA or study of organizational behavior or organizational design, or it can come from experience as a leader in multiple organizations.

As a consultant and coach, I have had insight to the cultures of several hundred organizations. As such, I am able to see themes across academic, government, and private sector organizations. This experience also informs what I don't know. Every organization and even every leader-driven entity can carry a unique culture.

In an organizational context, the coach's understanding of organization structures, systems, and cultures will assist their coaching. For example, perhaps a client is overwhelmed with work and unable to execute with a degree of quality that is expected. If a coach is unaware of the systemic approach often present within organizations, the coach might focus on the client's ability to organize and prioritize. If the coach is aware of the potential stakeholders and pressures in organizations, the coach might ask some of the following questions:

- What conversations have you had with your leader?

- Who is setting the expectations?

- What resources have you accessed to support your work?

- What are the quantity and quality of your relationships across the organization to complete the work?

It is impactful when the coach can engender system thinking or an enterprise approach in their client. Too often, leaders see their responsibilities from the point of view of their group or their division rather than from the point of view of the whole organization. The coach can grow the leader's perspective by asking how decisions they are making may impact all aspects of the organization. I refer to this as building the enterprise view.

When we talk about organization understanding, we are referring to a broad understanding of how systems or organizations in general operate. However, there are some who assume that a coach must understand the client's particular industry, company, or technical area. When coaching leaders, this level of specificity is generally not required knowledge at the commencement of the coaching. One of the problems with requiring a coach to know a great deal of specificity is that there may be a consulting expectation. The client may perceive the coach to be a consultant. Or the coach might enter the consulting space without allowing the client to decide on the options at hand. Coaches should be looking for ways to inform their understanding of a client's industry, company, or technical area; however, they should be clear that, when coaching, they do not provide consulting advice.

6   COACH INQUIRY ABSENT OF BIAS

Inquiry free of judgment or bias does not mean that coaches won't have judgment and bias. Instead, they are aware of these and put them aside for the benefit of the client. The coach may believe they have the "right" answer to a client dilemma, but that is irrelevant to the coaching conversation. It is the client's determination that leads. While the coach may share an opinion, it is always done as a possible option for the client to assess for themselves. This is an important distinction between coaching and advising, mentoring, or consulting. (Chapter 4 discusses these distinctions in depth.)

In my coaching, clients often bring up a "stay or go" conversation. Coaches may feel torn in their loyalty to the sponsor organization. However, by allowing the client to entertain this thought, it is often the case that the coaching leads to the client resolving issues in their current organization. My experience is the more a client can discuss leaving an organization, the more likely they are to stay.

COMMON BIASES IN COACHING

When coaching in organizations, there are certain areas that are more prone to bias. Here are a few types of scenarios in which I've observed these struggles take place:

Sponsor bias: While the coach honors and respects the sponsor organization, they are not responsible to the organization *when engaging in conversation with the client* in a way that inhibits the client thinking. The coaching conversation must be free of that bias until the client is making choices that may be contrary to the organization's interests. At that point, the coach engages the client in assessing how their choices may impact the organization.

This requires the client (not the coach) to own the impact of their decisions on the organization.

Leadership bias: Often, coaches come from a background in leadership. They can overlay their own biases from their previous experiences. They fail to realize that giving advice and "knowing what worked before" is not necessarily right for this client or this organization. Most importantly, the coach is taking away the ability of the client to think through options and determine what is right.

Internal coach bias: The internal coach can be subject to numerous challenges with bias. These are covered more deeply in chapter 10, which discusses Internal Coaching. Some of these include positional bias, which occurs when the client or coach has different power within the institution. Others deal with organization bias, which can take place when the coach advocates for specific outcomes due to their investment in the organization.

 ## 7   COACH COMFORT WITH EMOTIONS IN THE WORKPLACE

Coaching requires comfort with clients' emotions. If the conversations that are most transformative are ones that are really important for the client, then they will often carry emotional content. In conversations about leadership, leaders may relate deeply held convictions and values that drive their choices. Clients can become emotional when talking about these more profound sides of themselves. By bringing those experiences forward, clients can uncover values and emotions that drive choices.

When we discuss why a particular action or relationship is hard for a client, this topic can lead to strong emotions. Coaching on balancing complex personal and professional challenges, such as disease, grief, and job loss, contain strong emotions. These conversations require the coach to be able to provide an accepting and open environment for the client. It requires the coach to be both empathetic as well as separate from the shared emotion.

"If it doesn't challenge you,
it won't change you."
—FRED DEVITO, MIND-BODY ENTREPRENEUR

The coach manages these conversations in partnership with the client. For example, if the coaching is one of many meetings for the leader in the middle of the day and the conversation becomes emotional, the coach needs to partner with the client in managing the meeting, so the client is prepared to move on with their day. The coach may suggest a way to circle back to the conversation later at the end of the workday. Or they may take the meeting from a different location that is comfortable for the client.

As we've seen in this chapter, coaching in organizations to support organizational outcomes requires attention to a number of factors. When these are in place, the coaching is optimized for all the parties involved: coach, client, and organization. In the next chapter, I will discuss the different types of coaching that organizations can use to achieve their goals.

CHAPTER SUMMARY: AT A GLANCE

- Coaching in organizations requires special attention to seven areas including aligning to organizational goals, ownership of outcomes, confidentiality, and attention to client ownership of the outcomes, as well as coach enterprise view, inquiry absent of bias, and a comfort with emotions in the workplace.

- Providing clarity to the coach and client on organizational goals can be especially effective when it occurs at the beginning of the coaching engagement. This clarity remains an important element throughout the coaching.

- Ultimately, clients are responsible for the outcomes from the coaching. That must be a clear norm set at the beginning of each coaching engagement.

- Coaches must ensure a confidential and autonomous environment throughout the coaching; doing so provides a safe, trustworthy space where the client can grow.

- Coaches who understand how organizations function will be able to better inform their coaching conversations and action plans with clients.

- Maintaining an unbiased approach is essential for coaches to enable the client to create their needed solutions.

- Being comfortable with emotions is key in Human Challenge coaching, as it can lead to discovery and change.

Seven Coaching Types for Organizations

"Coaching isn't therapy. It's product
development, with you as the product."

—CLAIRE TRISTRAM IN *FAST COMPANY*

In the past, organizations frequently deployed a single type of coaching, which involved an individual coach and an individual client. The two would work together, focusing on the client's needs and performance. Organizations didn't typically use coaching to complement and achieve organizational outcomes.

As the profession of coaching has evolved and it has been used more strategically, new types of coaching have developed. Each type has a different impact for the organization. In this chapter, we'll consider seven of the main types of coaching available for organizations today. They are:

1   Individual optimization

2   Individual development and performance

3   Team optimization

4   Team work content

5   Teaching leaders and managers coaching skills

6   Group coaching

7   Peer coaching

Overall, these different types can be integrated into a portfolio solution. Some organizations seeking to create coaching cultures may deploy all these types of coaching at once. This is especially true for organizations that want to have the core competencies of change permeate the entire workforce. The following chart further outlines the goals of these types of coaching, along with the impact they can create.

7 Main Types of Coaching in Organizations

TYPE OF COACHING	Goal	Business Impact
INDIVIDUAL OPTIMIZATION	To support the client in "showing up" at work at their best through coaching on personal or professional topics	Client may resolve numerous barriers to their performance, creating an energized, optimistic, and empowered approach to their work.
INDIVIDUAL DEVELOPMENT AND PERFORMANCE	To develop skills or competencies	Client's professional and personal growth will be catalyzed.
TEAM OPTIMIZATION	To create a high-performing team	Team's professional and personal interactions will be of a positive and productive nature.
TEAM WORK CONTENT	To resolve strategic issues of the team	Team will arrive at decisions with a higher degree of quality and speed
TEACHING LEADERS AND MANAGERS COACHING SKILLS	Training leaders and managers to use skills they can deploy with their teams and reports	Create a coaching competency-based culture with growth mindset. A focus on others, listening, and powerful questions are present.
GROUP COACHING	Coaching a selected group of individuals that are not a team	Reach more individuals at once, creating economies of scale in the coaching.
PEER COACHING	To create a co-coaching environment with a group of individuals	Create a co-learning or peer learning environment for community building, as well as competency building.

In the following sections of this chapter, I'll further define each of these coaching types. As you read through each description, keep in mind that it is quite common to use more than one type within an organization. I invite you to envision scenarios in which several could work together in tandem to have a larger impact.

1 INDIVIDUAL OPTIMIZATION COACHING

This type of coaching focuses on strengthening the overall leader performance. The goals are often set by the client and can include work or life goals. Done well, this coaching builds the core competencies of change, including growth mindset and confidence in meeting change.

Some organizations make individual optimization coaching available to any employee who would like it. The end result to the organization is that they achieve a growth mindset culture. Other organizations target high potential and high-value leaders or high-performing leaders whose performance is lagging. In the case of the lagging performance client, the sponsor may know something is compromising the performance of the leader but suspect it has to do with a morale issue that the person is not sharing. For example, I once coached a client who was navigating a complex divorce at the start of our engagement. By allowing the client to process the emotional and logistic demands of this event, the client was able to better manage showing up at work with greater commitment and energy.

Individual optimization coaching is often employed for issues related to career satisfaction too. Often when clients first come to me, they are unclear about their future career development. They may be ready to leave their organization. Through our coaching, we frequently discuss how they can be proactive in crafting their careers within their organizations. As a result, a departure is often avoided.

THE IMPORTANCE OF INCORPORATING THE WHOLE LIFE AND WHOLE PERSON

In my experience with individual optimization coaching, I frequently implement a holistic approach. After meeting the executive who is to receive the coaching, we'll develop an agenda. It might include health, personal, and work goals that the client designs. The agenda doesn't have any organizational objectives other than enhancement of the executive's performance.

While the client focuses on key work competencies, they also see tremendous benefits from coaching on life balance or health issues. Once these matters are resolved through the coaching, the client is able to achieve significantly higher performance in the workplace. In fact, I've found that talent retention is profoundly positively impacted by coaching. It provides a safe space for the client to talk about and manage concerns about the workplace or personal issues that could have led them to leave the firm. The coaching can help uncover solutions that provide the client with a path to follow within the organization.

② INDIVIDUAL DEVELOPMENT AND PERFORMANCE COACHING

This type of coaching focuses on development of the manager or leader. It has the objective of enhancing the workplace competencies of the client. The goal of the engagement is often to adopt competencies that require generative learning such as emotional intelligence, conflict management, difficult conversations, and executive presence. Some organizations assign coaches at different levels of leadership when managers must adopt new skills to achieve higher levels of the organization. Or they recognize that an organizational change requires new mindsets as well as competencies and assign coaches to those who are impacted. Another strategy for deployment of development coaching is the integration of leadership training with coaching. By incorporating learning into the coaching process, the method holds an advantage over stand-alone training sessions. While training can introduce new knowledge, most of the lessons learned are lost if there is no accompanying coaching. Without coaching, there isn't an effective integration of the material into the leaders' lives in the workplace.

> **Without coaching, there isn't an effective integration of the material into the leaders' lives in the workplace.**

CASE ILLUSTRATION

Using Coaching with Training in an Academic Setting

As a leadership development coach for the Executive MBA program at the University of Maryland's Robert H. Smith School of Business, I coached students over the course of their studies. These coaching sessions were included as part of the curriculum. The students who attended the Executive MBA program were fully employed; as such, they took what they learned in theory in the classroom, worked with me to integrate theory into personal action, and then entered the learning loop of trial and error to perfect the learning.

During my time coaching these Executive MBA program students, we debriefed a number of style assessments. Through this exercise, we gained awareness of default approaches to work and learning. We then defined and coached against development objectives that were partially formed from the academic curriculum they were learning in the classroom.

148

Supervisor-aligned coaching is a technique used in development coaching. (See more on alignment meetings in chapter 8.) The sponsor (HR or supervisor), the client, and the coach cocreate the coaching goals. This provides the opportunity for the sponsor to set development goals with the client and coach. Goals can include both personal client goals and organizational goals. By aligning the client and supervisor, there is often buy-in to the client's development and increased support of the personal and professional goals. This helps create optimal performance through the partnership between the client and boss.

Depending on the sponsor, these alignment meetings may occur multiple times across the coaching engagement. They frequently take place at the midpoint and end of the coaching. It is important that the client—not the coach—leads the conversation, so that the client is forging the responsibility for their own growth and sharing those elements of the coaching that don't violate any areas they want to keep private.

3   TEAM OPTIMIZATION

This type of coaching involves a team and its leader and aims to achieve better internal team performance. With clients, the coach might work to help them improve team communication dynamics and decision-making systems. This form of coaching can involve team facilitation, as well as one-on-one coaching with the team leader and individual team members. Ideally, the coach works closely with the team leader to ensure alignment with the leader's goals.

Typically, the coach first meets with the team leader to understand the leader's goals for the team. These objectives might include greater collaboration, conflict resolution, and optimized communication. The coach uncovers the leader's perceptions of the team dynamics, norms, and culture. The coach then uses this information to prepare for the research phase.

In the research phase, the coach interviews the team members and team stakeholders to assess the strengths and weaknesses of the team. The coach evaluates the team's communication channels, morale, work patterns, and relationships. A picture of the areas of strengths and weaknesses is assessed, and a summary (which doesn't reveal sources) is presented to the leader to design the optimization coaching process.

At this point, the leader may need coaching to absorb some of the feedback. This is often required if the leader feels the evaluation is critical of their leadership. Generally, however, I find that if the leader has welcomed the coaching process, they are eager to learn and grow with their team.

The agenda for one or more team facilitations, along with a plan for any one-on-one coaching with team members, is established. In the team facilitations, the coach strives to engender the same personal accountability and empowerment that they create in an individual coaching engagement. This is done by facilitating a learning loop experience in which the team processes a structured series of issues and questions. They reflect on their learnings and then articulate next steps. In between facilitations, the team may have individual coaching to assist them with integrating these next steps. When the team meets again, they hold each other accountable and assess their progress as a group.

In their book, *Immunity to Change*, Robert Kegan and Lisa Laskow Lahey delve into team optimization coaching.[12] They explain how they work with teams and use a specific optimization process. Their method uncovers what they refer to as the "hidden agendas" to change. The hidden agendas are the commitments we make to other values or beliefs that hinder our ability to adopt new behaviors.

CASE ILLUSTRATION

Coaching Teams to Transition to New Leadership

I once coached a technology group that had just received a new leader. The team had been "stuck" in a mental model of how they worked together that the previous leader had established. These norms led to behaviors of blame and finger-pointing. It also created an absence of ownership to team outcomes.

We started the engagement with interviews that uncovered the behaviors that were inhibiting the team to work effectively and even civilly with each other. We worked closely with the team leader to design several phases of team coaching and facilitation. We created a goal of setting new communication norms.

Through various facilitated exercises, we were able to "name" the mental model and associated communication norms in the old way of doing business as a team. Then we defined what new norms and thinking were required for a better model. We implemented those with the collaboration of the group leaders.

Clearly, the adoption of these norms required the team members to build generative learning processes to try out the new behaviors. They then perfected these behaviors with the different styles of their colleagues. Having open communication and ownership that assisted the team in engaging in a learning loop required trust. They needed to know that their colleagues wouldn't issue blame for mistakes.

Through our coaching, the team arrived at the early stages of developing greater trust and accountability for the team shared-outcomes. Being able to identify the old norms and set new norms helped them move away from their previous behaviors. They could set up better work patterns more freely and develop a mindset that allowed for further learning and growth.

4   TEAM WORK CONTENT

In this type of team coaching, the focus is on the work product of the team. The coaching is directed to a more tactical problem, but it will often contain the need to work with generative processes. Team work content coaching uses generative learning techniques to assist the team in doing their work. The facilitator will often be a technical expert who engages in the work of the team with them.

CASE ILLUSTRATION

A Team Uses Coaching to Better Understand and Approach Their Workload

A team came to me for coaching to help them with their team work content. They were struggling to maintain accountability and focus on their deliverables. They had an overwhelm of projects that they collectively oversaw, yet they had little understanding of how one project impacted another. For instance, one project led by the finance department influenced another project initiative led by the IT department, but there was little cross-department communication or alignment or priority setting from leadership.

The team work content coaching program I developed for the team included both team facilitation and individual coaching. We had a series of facilitations to clarify—as a team—all the projects and how they potentially dovetailed or influenced other projects. In between these meetings, team members had "homework." They queried their subordinates for more detail of how they interfaced with other departments. They shared the information they gathered during their "homework" assignments in the facilitated meetings. In essence, the team was gaining greater awareness of what they did and how they did it.

Once there was more clarity with the projects, we held a facilitated meeting that outlined new processes and norms of how the team would work together going forward. One-on-one sessions assisted individual members to overcome their resistance to the group-focused priorities. In my coaching, I observed that some individuals needed to find new ways to express their needs to the team. Others had to overcome turf protection mentality and identify a new team-focused alliance.

As a result of the facilitation meetings and one-on-one coaching, the team was able to better understand their project load and its implications. They learned ways to approach the newly set processes and norms. Overall, they were equipped to handle their workload in a more productive, communicative, and informed way.

5   TEACHING LEADERS AND MANAGERS COACHING SKILLS

Many organizations are now enrolling their leaders and managers in coaching training or coaching skills training. When leaders and managers have the ability to use coaching skills, the benefits reach beyond the specific adoption of skills. This skill set can also help to build a culture. The "coaching culture" is one that has the core competencies of change consisting of a growth mindset, agility with change, and a focus on people and empowering people. In this culture, personal and professional growth are valued. Mistakes are simply part of the learning loop. This approach is vital for organizations that face change on a regular basis as most do.

> The "coaching culture" is one that has the core competencies of change consisting of a growth mindset, agility with change, and a focus on people and empowering people.

Many mentor programs also train their mentors in coaching skills to enhance their impact. This allows the mentorship to carry out more than pure advice-giving. It can include competencies in building the mentee's ability to formulate solutions on their own.

6   GROUP COACHING

In this type of coaching, several individuals work with a coach to tackle developmental and optimization issues. For example, an organization may target a population of newly promoted individuals who are supervising people for the first time. The group of new supervisors might be presented training materials on how to deliver feedback or deal with difficult conversations. The coach will work with the group to assist with the integration of the material and bring forth contributions from the whole group thinking to enrich the process.

While being coached individually is often preferable so that the unique barriers for one person to adoption are quickly assessed and addressed, this form of group coaching can have certain benefits. It typically lends to building community within the organization. In addition, group members learn from each other during the coaching.

7   PEER COACHING

This type of coaching involves a group of peers who come together to co-coach each other. Some oversight of the group by a coach is beneficial to assist them with coaching processes of inquiry, listening, nonjudgment, and mindset. I have witnessed a successful paradigm used in an organization in which an internal coach oversaw the peer coaching program. They visited the peer coaching sessions regularly. The HR professional observed and coached the group on how to approach issues in a coaching capacity of enhanced thinking rather than only sharing how-to material.

As we've seen, the world of coaching today has matured to include different applications of coaching and coaching skills. Organizations now have a wide selection of coaching types they can use to pursue organizational goals. Mixing types of coaching may be the right solution for a company undergoing change, transition, or looking to take on new competitive advantages within its industry.

CHAPTER SUMMARY: AT A GLANCE

- Historically, coaching in an organization was viewed as an arrangement between one coach and one client. That has changed, and organizations now have many coaching types available to them to build a strategic coaching program.

- There are seven main types of coaching available today: individual optimization, individual development and performance, team optimization, team work content, group coaching, teaching leaders and managers coaching skills, and peer coaching.

- Individual optimization coaching focuses on human potential in general.

- Individual development and performance coaching has a focus on integrating competencies and skills to enhance performance.

- Team optimization coaching looks for ways to improve overall internal team performance.

- Team work content coaching delves into increasing a team's performance and function within an organization by facilitating their work.

- Teaching leaders and managers coaching skills can improve the overall company environment and performance in change and create a coaching culture.

- Group coaching engages a small group (not a team) of individuals with a coach that provides benefits of learning from each other. The coach ensures that the engagement is not advice-giving but rather exploration and learning.

- Peer coaching consists of a peer group that co-coaches each other. Ideally, they are overseen by a coach or the group is trained in coaching to ensure conversations are open, co-learning environments.

- Organizations may implement several types of coaching into a strategic portfolio of coaching types, depending on their specific desired outcomes and budget.

CHAPTER 8

Techniques and Technology Tools for Aligning Coaching to Organization Outcomes

---

"It is action that creates motivation."

—STEVE BACKLEY, OLYMPIC ATHLETE

J ust as I've observed coaching grow and change during the last two decades, I've also watched the tools available for coaching increase. Today, there are a plethora of techniques and technology tools that can be used to coach within an organization. Collectively, they can be used to ensure the organization outcomes are incorporated into the coaching engagement.

In this chapter, I'll cover some of the main techniques and technology tools that can help align the coaching to the organization goals. I'll first explain two coaching techniques, which are the alignment meeting and the 360 feedback. I'll also explain some of the forward-looking technology tools that are, in part, driving the move toward more use of coaching and more strategic use of coaching. I'll discuss several innovations in the technology field that can be integrated into a strategic coaching program.

THE ALIGNMENT MEETING

In coaching engagements with an individual, a key to ensure a strategic use of coaching is to create alignment with organizational goals through the alignment session. The alignment session is a coach-facilitated conversation with the client and their sponsor. The sponsor is either the client's supervisor or another professional who oversees the client's growth and development or organizational outcomes. Alignment meetings most often occur at the beginning of the coaching sessions. They may also occur at a midpoint and at the end of the coaching engagement.

The purpose of an alignment session is often stated as an opportunity to incorporate the supervisor's input to the client coaching goals and to have the client share their goals and progress with the supervisor. However, an alignment session has far more benefits that enhance both the sponsor leadership and the client coaching goals. These benefits include:

- Coaching goals alignment and feedback

- Articulation of success for the coaching by the supervisor

- Enhancing the role of the supervisor as development advocate

- Increased client self-advocacy

In the following sections, we'll take a closer look at each of these benefits that can come from an alignment meeting.

Coaching Goals Alignment and Feedback

Alignment between the client, sponsor, and coach on what will be tackled by the client in the sessions is beneficial to the success of the coaching. Since coaching is confidential, engaging the supervisor in reviewing the client's goals allows the supervisor to add to or revise the goals. This may reveal unstated agendas by the supervisor. For example, the supervisor may find delivering critical feedback difficult. By engaging in a positive conversation positioned as how to "enhance the client's learning for continued growth," the supervisor may be able to express what they hesitated to express before.

The clearer the supervisor's expectations are of the client, the more likely the client will be successful in fulfilling them. If the supervisor is deploying organization resources to the client's development and growth with coaching,

> **The clearer the supervisor's expectations are of the client, the more likely the client will be successful in fulfilling them.**

this helps the supervisor feel that the investment is achieving their leadership objectives as well. The coach can pose the question, "What would be success in your (the supervisor's) eyes for the client at the end of this coaching assignment?" This question can unearth any unspoken agendas or expectations that the supervisor may have for the client. It can expose any unrealistic expectations the supervisor may have for the coaching. For example, the supervisor may say they want the coach and client to work on a strategy document deliverable. This allows the coach to explain to the supervisor the definition of coaching as assisting the client in the ability to execute on that; however, the coaching doesn't involve consulting the client on that matter.

In the coaching program models of Audience-Target Outcomes and Organizational-Target Outcomes Coaching, there are organizational goals for the coaching that are communicated in the alignment meeting. (See more on coaching program models in chapter 9.) These may be to instill certain leadership competencies or to integrate new learnings or other various outcomes desired by the organization. In this case, the alignment meeting ensures that the coach and client have connected the client goals to the organizational expectations. The meeting with the sponsor or supervisor will be for the client to express their unique goals for the coaching as translated into what barriers or challenges they face in adopting the changes required by the organization strategy. For example, if the organization has asked decision-making to be delegated down to the next level of management, that will be the umbrella goal stated by the client and coach. However, under that umbrella, there will be goals the client feels they need to achieve to accomplish the umbrella goal. The client may say they will need to work on communication skills specific to delegation. They might also say they will need to enhance their strategic visioning and communication to better articulate outcomes and delegate.

Often, clients perceive that the supervisor defines their success as financial goals alone. That said, employees who achieve financial goals may fail to gain promotions because the manager has never effectively shared other deliverables they want from the employee. Thus, the alignment meeting is a process of searching for the unspoken metrics for success, so the client is not blindsided.

For example, the supervisor may say they would like the manager to work on their delegation skills. The reason they give may be so that the manager can increase the team output and step up to more leadership skills, such as defining and driving strategy. It may come as a surprise to the employee that defining strategy was an expectation of the supervisor. Even the supervisor may not have thought to articulate this expectation to the client before.

Additionally, the client may ask the coach to pose a question to the supervisor. The coach might inquire, "What are the priority deliverables that you expect from your client over the next six months?" While that should have been a conversation that was held between the supervisor and client before, it may give the supervisor a new perspective on their response as they describe it to a third party.

I often find that the supervisor doesn't know how to provide feedback on soft skills such as emotional intelligence or communication in a way that feels comfortable. In the alignment meeting, the coach can model how to tease out the vocabulary used in framing improvements in an effective way. For example, the supervisor may say the employee needs to have better "optics" with top leadership. This is an unclear objective: it is ambiguous what the issue is behind that comment and what behaviors the leader would want to see. Does the leader think the employee doesn't express themselves clearly? Is it that they don't speak enough in meetings? Do they fail to tout their successes adequately? The coach asks questions to help clarify what the leader means. The coach might inquire the following:

- "What behaviors would you see if the employee were to ensure better optics with leadership?"

- "When you say 'leadership,' who do you mean?"

- "What benefits would it bring to you and the employee by having better optics?"

As the supervisor answers these questions, the client is able to better understand what the expectations are. They can then work with the coach to begin the improvement process.

Enhancing the Role of the Supervisor as Development Advocate

The alignment meeting provides an opportunity for a supervisor to shift away from transactional communication of the day-to-day needs of the operation to a focus on developing the client. These client-development-focused conversations often are not planned, and when there is not a precedent for them, leaders often don't know how to jump-start them. The alignment meeting can set a precedent for continuing feedback to the client based on their professional development.

Through the alignment meeting, the supervisor is learning how to articulate professional development objectives and build out behaviors attributed to those objectives. The coach may hear the supervisor use work goals as coaching goals such as, "I expect him to merge the two teams by Q3." The coach may ask, "What strengths and challenges do you think the client will bring to doing this?" The question frames the work objective on the professional development opportunities.

For supervisors who are well versed in professional development work, the challenge of providing regular feedback to their people is that they don't assign the time to do it. The alignment sessions are an opportunity for the supervisor or client to recognize that feedback is indeed important, and that a meeting about it can be positive and productive. The coach can ensure that the supervisor and client have a next step in place to make these types of meetings regular events. This is often done through questions. The coach might ask, "How will you make this type of conversation a regular part of the work over the next year?"

If a final alignment session is conducted at the end of the coaching assignment, the coach can pose the question of how the client can receive professional development support going forward. This question evokes thinking in the supervisor about what their role might be going forward. The client and supervisor can be encouraged to articulate their next steps after the coaching terminates.

Increased Client Self-Advocacy

The alignment meeting can enhance the client's ability to self-advocate. Often, an employee is hesitant to ask their supervisor for support. They may have secret ambitions to move up through the organization but not share these with their supervisor. They may struggle with developing certain skills and competencies and not think to ask for assistance. In my coaching, I hear reasoning such as "My leader is so busy; I don't want to burden them," or "I don't want to appear unskilled in front of my boss."

In each alignment meeting, I ask my clients what support they would like to receive from their supervisor. The approach seems to give the client a feeling of safety in asking for support from the leader. Once they see a positive reaction on the part of the leader, they find they can continue to advocate for themselves in the future. Additionally, this method helps the client shift away from driving through their day without picking up their head to thinking about other questions they might ask for themselves.

For more on how to conduct alignment meetings go to linktr.ee/sandrastewart.com.

360 FEEDBACK

360 feedback is researching perceptions about the client being coached (team or individual) from leaders, peers, and reports and sometimes other stakeholders. In my work, I frequently recommend

360 feedback to align an individual or team with organizational goals and expectations. When clients receive feedback of their performance from individuals they impact, they are able to better identify what strengths they bring, as well as what enhancements are needed to perform their job. The coach is also better able to partner with the client in aligning what the client can work on with the organizational goals.

The 360 feedback may be quantitative, such as a survey of a robust sample of individuals that is computed with statistically analyzed data. It might also be qualitative. In this case, it consists of interviews conducted by the coach or others and then summarized in a bullet point or narrative form.

The quantitative 360 requires set questions with a multiple-choice response. It might also include some open-ended questions. The benefit of the quantitative measurement is the ability to reach a larger number of respondents quickly and to gain a quantitative performance metric. When the report is issued, it is possible for the client to see where they score high and where they score relatively low. With these results, they can target their coaching efforts.

It is, however, not advisable to use these metrics to benchmark leaders across the organization with each other. There are three key reasons for this:

- The environment impacts a leader's perceived performance (e.g., a toxic division leader can drive lower scores for the leader below them).

- Respondents are different across leaders, so the scoring populations differ.

- Interpretation of a competency such as "technical knowledge" could be irrelevant for one leader and crucial for another.

One quantitative assessment, The Leadership Profile, has created a leader benchmark based on leaders across all organizations that allows a leader to compare themselves to a leader profile developed from a long study of high-performing leaders. This assessment can provide a fairer benchmark. The leader charts their progress over time with that of an external standard.

The qualitative 360 are interviews conducted by the coach or third party. They can be tailored to the leader or team being coached. Most coaching engagements use interviews as a means to help the client gain self-awareness. This technique provides the following key benefits:

- The questions in the interviews can be tailored to the particular concerns conveyed by other sources, such as a quantitative assessment, a leader, or the client's own curiosity.

- The interviewer can ask the respondent for examples and definitions to build deeper understanding of their comments.

- The interviewer asks for behaviors that build meaning in comments such as "They have bad communication," which on their own can be far too general.

- The interviewer can pick up on emotional content that surveys cannot elicit, thereby identifying the depth of the impact.

To provide candid feedback, the coach should adhere to a few logistics. First, the list of interviewees can be vetted by the client's supervisor to ensure a good sample of respondents. Second, the client sends an email asking for the candid feedback of the respondents in service to their growth and indicates that the results will be shared only with the client and not their leaders. Third, the interviewer ensures that the respondents know that nothing will be attributed. This means that the interviewer will not reveal individual comments and the identity of the respondent. Instead, the interviewer will report only themes across all respondents.

> ## ONGOING FEEDBACK: PULSE SURVEYS AND INTERVIEWS
>
> Pulse surveys and interviews are another important form of aligning the original goals of the coaching with the coaching engagement. Pulse surveys and interviews that occur after six months or more of the coaching engagement can gather feedback on changes in the client. Generative change can take time. Furthermore, the perceptions that others have of a client may also need time to evolve—even when the client's behavior has changed.

TECHNOLOGY TOOLS

Technology is playing an important role in the way coaching is carried out. It both enables a wider use of coaching and encourages a more strategic approach to coaching. Some of the common technology tools available today include: coaching management platforms, coach-scaling organizations, assessments used by coaches, websites to connect clients with coaches, behavior modification and leadership training apps, training platforms, and coach business management websites.

In the following sections, I'll briefly describe each one.

Coaching Program Management Platforms

These technology tools are a way to manage multiple coaches and coaching types across an organization and are often needed to achieve a broad scale of coaching. These platforms have a centralized system to facilitate the pairing of coaches to teams and individuals, track coaching engagements, and maintain a library of materials used in coaching engagements.

With a coaching program management platform, a CPS, coach manager, or coordinator can more easily oversee the deployment of the coaches. They can launch the coach and client with materials consistent with all coach pairings created for a specific organizational objective. They ensure processes such as plan development and alignment meetings are tracked. The platform can also collect historical data to see which individuals and teams have experienced what coaching initiatives over time.

Coach-Scaling Organizations

Coach-scaling organizations (CSOs) are organizations that have a portfolio of coaches that an organization can access, so they don't have to maintain their own coach roster. Some of these CSOs also provide a strategic consulting approach at the design phase of a coaching engagement. They work with the client to articulate their desired organizational outcomes from coaching and then assist them in material development and coach pairing that fits that strategic objective. Optify is an example of a CSO that provides their clients with a strategic consultative entry point to their coaching program. They ask their clients what their end goal is from the coaching. Then, they tailor both the coaching plan and the materials to work toward that goal. They vet and hire a stable of coaches and then use an online software system that pairs the coaches and clients, houses the materials specific to any number of targeted coaching engagements, embeds surveys to get feedback on the coaching quality and progress, and ties into results of the coaching as perceived by others.

CASE ILLUSTRATION

A Start-Up Uses Optify to Achieve Organizational Goals

A CEO of a start-up approached Optify for coaching services. During its initial stages, the firm didn't have the funds or orientation to engage in talent development. After undergoing fast growth and development, the start-up wanted to invest in their people. The company had two main business objectives:

1. Attract and retain the best talent in the industry by demonstrating their investment in their growth.

2. Create an entrepreneurial culture.

Optify held meetings with several leaders in the start-up to identify behaviors and competencies of the entrepreneurial leader. Using this as a reference, Optify developed a coaching program to suit the organization. This led to the development of a coaching program that dovetailed with training to embed this in the organization.

Assessments Used by Coaches

Many organizations choose a particular online assessment to view leadership style and competencies throughout the organization. Target Training International provides a number of DISC-based assessments. These help internal or external coaches to coach individuals and teams on work and communication style. The Leadership Circle Profile is a benchmarked 360 instrument that can view a leader's style with relationship to a top leader standard.

The results of an individual assessment not only help that leader develop competencies; they also allow the organization to see leadership competencies across the organization and identify gaps for specific teams or divisions. Some coach management platforms are now integrating assessments into their technology platform and seeking ways to use the assessment results in designing training and coaching programs.

Websites to Connect Clients with Coaches

There are internet sites that enable individuals or organizations to find a coach. A trusted space is the International Coaching Federation (ICF) coach referral site. All the coaches listed on this site are trained and credentialed. They have over 130 hours of training with ICF accredited institutions, and they have enough coaching experience to reach the various levels of coaching standards: Associate Certified Coach (ACC), Professional Certified Coach (PCC), and Master Certified Coach (MCC).

These sites are a good way for organizations to draw from a worldwide database of coaches. Many organizations have needs for coaches that are geographically in the location of their clients. Others require specific cultural understanding and language skills.

Access resources related to coaching in organizations at QR Code and link: linktr.ee/sandrastewart.com.

Behavior Modification and Leadership Training Apps

Apps that can be tailored and downloaded on your phone can assist as a reminder mechanism for behavior change and provide just-in-time learning materials. One example of this is the Leadx app. A Leadx representative works with the client organization to articulate the areas of desired competencies and behaviors. Then, they identify personality or behavior assessments that the organization would like to use to tailor the coaching plans for the individual. For example, the organization may want to build skills for their new supervisors in team management. Leadx would use the style or personality assessment data to tailor a learning and action program for each participant involving some key team management skills. If the participant is an extrovert or introvert, the app would tailor the plan for that style.

The Leadx app delivers micro learnings such as TED Talks, articles, podcasts, and other materials to the targeted individuals that teach team management. The app then builds a development plan for the participant for a time period consistent with the skill development. Nudges are sent to the individual through the app at desired time intervals. These notifications remind the participant about the plan and provide actions to take. When paired with a 360 assessment, Leadx has found significant improvement in the development of the targeted skill areas.

Habatica.com and PocketConfidant.com are two other habit trackers. There are also mood tracker apps. These can be used to build emotional intelligence, as they assist in building greater awareness of an individual's moods and their impact on performance.

Training Platforms

Training platforms provide single-site access to training materials and a coach-driven experience. For instance, LeaderJam.com allows organizations to manage training and coaching all in one platform. In this setup, the coach and client can meet and access the coach's training material and classes, as well as Leaderjam's curated materials.

Other sites provide leadership and soft skills training with coaching integrated into the package. Some of these include Wiley's CrossKnowledge.com and Everwise.com. The platform can be dropped into an organization's existing training program. Some coaching sites provide coaching for specific needs such as career coaching. KFAdvance.com assists individuals with tools and coaching to help them advance their career within or outside their organization.

Coach Business Management Websites

Individual coaches can provide single-site engagement management with technologies such as Coachmetrix.com and Vcita.com. They offer billing, scheduling, tracking, and communication systems to make it easier for coaches to conduct all these diverse tasks as a part of their business. Some include ways to share development plans and training materials in one place.

In this chapter, we've seen a glimpse of the techniques and recent innovations that currently help support coaching strategically within an organization. These techniques and tools will most certainly evolve quickly in coming years. A potential end state for technology in building human capital in organizations could be a total solution model that identifies development areas, records training and coaching participation, and tracks performance throughout the life span of the employee.

CHAPTER SUMMARY: AT A GLANCE

- Organizations can implement various techniques and technology tools to help align coaching to the organization goals.

- Two of the main techniques include the alignment meeting and the 360 feedback.

- The alignment meeting involves the coach, client, and supervisor. It can be used to not only tie the coaching to the organizational goals but also to reap more benefits for the client and supervisor, including enhanced self-advocacy, supervisor development focus, and growth mindset culture.

- The 360 feedback involves quantitative or qualitative surveys that can be used to help an individual or team client to identify their strengths and areas of improvement. This creates alignment with organizational goals and expectations.

- Some of the innovative technology tools available today include: coaching management platforms that manage multiple coaching engagements, coach-scaling organizations that provide program strategy and management, coaching assessments that create a common language of awareness, websites to connect clients with coaches, behavior modification apps, training platforms, and coach business management websites.

- These techniques and tools can be used to help support a coaching program that is strategically aligned to organization goals.

CHAPTER 9

Coaching Program Impact Models and Examples

"We don't mature through age;
we mature in awareness."
—BYRON KATIE, SPEAKER AND AUTHOR

As we have seen in earlier chapters, there are different types of coaching, including individual optimization and development, team optimization and work content, peer and group coaching, and teaching coaching skills to leaders. There are also tools that ensure alignment to organizational goals such as alignment meetings, feedback mechanisms, and specialized technology platforms.

In addition to the types and tools of coaching, there are different coaching models that define the target for the coaching based on the desired organizational outcomes. The targets range from smaller in scope—such as one person or one team—to populations of employees representing different positional levels, issue targets, or learning and development needs. They can even extend to a large-scale organization-wide target that spans across multiple populations. The coaching program strategy would articulate the desired outcomes from the coaching program. It would include the tools, types of coaching we outlined in previous chapters, and the impact models that we will discuss here.

In this chapter, I'll share an in-depth look at each model. I'll also provide an example that demonstrates the model at work. By the end of the chapter, you'll have a greater understanding of how these models function—and how they can be used to achieve desired organizational outcomes.

THE THREE COACHING PROGRAM IMPACT MODELS

The main models are Individual-Target, Audience-Target, and Organization-Target. Each model has a different level of impact and scope. As such, the amount of oversight and leadership strategy setting and involvement will vary, depending on which model is used. Here's an overview of the three models:

The Individual-Target: This model focuses on a single person's performance or a team's performance. It is designed to impact those who are coached during the coaching program. At the same time, the outcome of this type of coaching program model will have an exponential impact on the teams and individuals surrounding the clients.

The Audience-Target: With this model, there are specific strategic organizational outcomes for targeted groups of individuals within a company. The organization creates a strategic goal for a select group of leaders, managers, or employees. For example, audience targets can include seniority levels in the company related to leadership development competency development, or it could include audiences facing specific issues that would benefit from coaching. This might be high stress caused by a specific organizational change. It could also involve transition audiences, such as new hires or promotion and succession candidates. This model has a broader impact on multiple individuals and/or teams and accomplishes set strategic objectives.

The Organization-Target: This kind of model is used to carry out overarching, strategic, desired organizational outcomes. Coaching becomes the catalyst to organizational change that helps break down barriers to change and support the complex thinking and learning loop required. Within the model, there may be multiple target populations of individuals and teams that will be involved in creating the desired organizational outcomes. Given this larger view and scope, top leadership is more involved with the coaching program. A CPS or executive who has experience with building a coaching strategy is usually deployed to oversee the model.

The following chart outlines these three coaching program models. It also lists examples of the desired organizational outcomes they typically support. The chart identifies who is usually involved with each model and the strategy with which it often aligns.

Three coaching program impact models

COACHING PROGRAM MODEL	INDIVIDUAL-TARGET	AUDIENCE-TARGET	ORGANIZATION-TARGET
Strategic Organizational Outcomes Examples	Individual or team optimization and development	Retention of targeted populations Catalyzing leadership development for certain leadership levels Transition support Teaching and integrating skills and behaviors	Business integration of technologies, new systems, and processes Catalyzing business model changes such as mergers, matrix Culture and behavior change such as catalyzing innovation Retention of diversity on a large scale
Coaching Program Management	Coaching Program coordinator Facilitates client and coach communications	Coaching Program Manager or Strategist Builds coaching program strategy Manages coaching deployment and processes Designs and oversees quality control Maintains Coaching Cohort relationships	Senior Leadership signs off on Coaching Program Strategy
Senior Leadership Involvement* **This may vary by organization.*	None to some oversight	Senior Leadership signs off on Coaching Program Strategy	Leadership team includes Coaching Strategy Leader or Coaching Strategy Leadership is engaged in key leadership systems and processes
Strategy	Support and develop and optimize individuals and teams	Support and develop key target populations	Institute strategic organization growth or change

THE INDIVIDUAL-TARGET COACHING PROGRAM IMPACT MODEL

As its name implies, the Individual-Target Coaching Program Model is used to address individual coaching needs. There is usually a request for this type of coaching from a single executive or team. The organization goal in this model is to provide a leader or team coaching to support optimal performance and build the core competencies of change inherent in coaching engagements.

Through the Individual-Target Coaching Program Model, an employee may elect the coaching to become a better leader. The client and coach might create structure with the coaching to achieve that goal. For instance, they could conduct a work style assessment, or the coach might carry out interviews with others about the employee. In addition, the coach and client could have a launch meeting with the HR representative or the client's supervisor (or both) to align development goals for the coaching. In this sense, others might influence the coaching goals of the program. The client, however, drives the focus.

I frequently see this model offered by supervisors to their employees. For instance, a leader might know that an employee is under personal or work-related stress. The leader may feel it is not their area of expertise, or appropriate from their position, to discuss these issues with the individual. Certainly, it would be hard for the leader to spend time discussing marital discord or family illness with an employee to help them build coping strategies. The process takes time, diplomacy skills, and coaching skills, which the leader may not have. By offering a coach to help the employee through the stress-causing event, the employee can better manage the concern and still conduct their

By offering a coach to help the employee through the stress-causing event, the employee can better manage the concern and still conduct their job.

job. This setup engenders goodwill on the part of the employee toward the supervisor and organization. The employee recognizes their leader and organization have invested not only in their output but also their overall well-being.

In addition, a team leader might bring in a coach to help their team deal with underlying issues. For instance, the team leader might recognize a decrease in harmony or productivity within their team. The team may be struggling to reconcile different styles and maintain positive norms of communication and cooperation. When a coach works with the team, these teams can transform. They can shift from a low-performing, unhappy state into a high-performing, collaborative team. Any team has multiple stakeholders that depend upon that team to perform their own work. When the team improves, the stakeholders around the team improve as well. This creates an exponential benefit for the organization.

AN INDIVIDUAL-TARGET COACHING PROGRAM MODEL EXAMPLE

For about a decade, I worked with a coaching firm that deployed a one-year individual optimization program. This program provided a twelve-month coaching engagement, which was supported by a thought-provoking "curriculum." The arrangement assisted each client in exploring leadership competencies with assessment-guided goal setting, along with specific articles to evoke thinking on communication, relationship development, and life balance.

A particularly important segment in this engagement centered on values and their application to leadership. Another segment on health included stress management techniques, diet and nutrition tips, and sleeping guidelines. It also covered exercise, and each client had ten sessions with a personal trainer.

Organizations used this program for different strategic reasons, based on their overall needs and their employees' individual circumstances. In most cases, firms awarded the program to executives, according to their level of seniority and based on perceived needs. I often saw the program offered to the following individuals:

- A leader who took on significant new responsibilities. In this case, the individual often needed to revisit the concept of themselves and their leadership role.

- A high performer who was still performing but seemed especially tired or stressed.

- A leader who the organization felt deserved recognition and support.

In addition, companies and nonprofits often used this program when they went through the following types of circumstances:

- A reorganization that created a new team of members who operated under new leadership.

- A transition to matrix leadership.

- A global expansion that created a new cadre of leaders.

- A new initiative that required leaders to act more as consultants and salespeople to external customers.

During my decade at the company, I worked with a diverse mix of clients in different areas of their company. In most cases, I noticed the health aspect of the program turned out to be a remarkable generator of both leader performance and strong goodwill toward the company. Leaders felt the personal nature of the company wanting them to be healthy in body, mind, and life balance wedded them even more to the organization. One study by the coaching firm found retention to be above average for the company as a whole.

Personally, I often had conversations with my clients around the option of leaving their company. During those sessions, the client was able to see that what they wanted was, more often than not, available to them at that same company. They either were fearful to ask for what they wanted or failed to understand what they needed. The client also found that coaching through difficult bosses, circumstances, and job demands resulted in being able to resolve the dissatisfactions they had with the company. The coaching impacted job satisfaction and engagement with their company. It also grew their optimism and sense of possibilities for the future.

"The only person you are destined to become is the person you decide to be."

—RALPH WALDO EMERSON, ESSAYIST, LECTURER, PHILOSOPHER, ABOLITIONIST, AND POET

THE AUDIENCE-TARGET COACHING PROGRAM IMPACT MODEL

This model includes organizational objectives for the coaching and is targeted to specific populations or issues. A variety of different organizational priorities may help form the desired organizational outcomes for the coaching. For instance, this model is often used for targeting specific audiences undergoing significant change or targeted audiences for leadership training and development, promotion coaching, and transition coaching.

Some organizations use this model for key leadership level transitions that their employees encounter. In these cases, coaching may be important to catalyze the employees' mastery of the new expectations that come with their new roles. For example, a company might provide coaches for employees moving from a senior manager position to a partner, from a manager to leader, or a leader to executive. The client's leadership competencies in the new position are not yet developed. The goal is to catalyze this development process through the learning loop of coaching.

This model can be used for personal transitions as well. For instance, an organization may use coaching to reintegrate employees who left the workplace to care for children or elderly relatives. Upon reentering, the employees might need to reestablish themselves or enter into a different job. Coaching can help the employees manage any ongoing conflicts of life balance and address the difficult process of gaining credibility and momentum at work.

The Audience-Target model might also be integrated with training. Talent management professionals often build strategies to enhance the skills of their employees. They may use coaching to help the student population integrate the learning into their workplace. For example, if the training materials include building soft skills of emotional intelligence, the coach may work with the employee on their understanding of the concepts within their work. In this case, the coach and client identify where the client is most challenged by the Emotional Intelligence framework. They build action plans on shoring up areas of weakness.

For team coaching, organizations may choose specific categories of teams or moments in a team's evolution to deploy coaching. For example, a team audience target may be teams that newly form or are charged with entrepreneurial or quick-change goals. The need for these teams to perform at a high level quickly qualifies them for team coaching. An organization may target international and virtual teams to receive optimization coaching to enhance team performance. Best-practice training on culture sensitivity or virtual team management might become part of the coaching program.

> "Tell me and I forget, teach me and I may remember, involve me and I learn."
> —BENJAMIN FRANKLIN, WRITER, POLITICAL PHILOSOPHER, POLITICIAN, SCIENTIST, HUMORIST, AND CIVIC ACTIVIST

In my years of coaching, I have often found organizations targeting leadership development to specific audiences. This is typically the most common way that the Audience-Target model is used. Under this design, the coaching can be effective for both the leaders involved and the overall organization.

AN AUDIENCE-TARGET COACHING PROGRAM MODEL EXAMPLE

Deltek, a global software and solutions company with over three thousand employees worldwide, sought to strengthen its talent benchmark. The firm's leadership wanted to use the coaching to complement HR's development efforts in succession planning, mentorship, and growth of emerging talent.

The company initially introduced coaching to its top executives at the senior VP level and above. To do this, Deltek used externally sourced coaches. The firm found coaching to be so effective that it decided to expand its efforts. The vice president of HR, Hope Needham, a trained and certified coach, worked with her leadership to craft a coaching and leadership development program. The intent was to catalyze the adoption of leadership competencies throughout the company. Her plan included giving every employee in the company access to coaching and automated talent development.

- Once developed, the program offered:
- External executive coaching for senior-level executives
- External one-on-one virtual coaching for the director level
- Dedicated internal coaching via trained coaching staff for managers and above
- Enterprise-wide, AI-driven leadership "coaching" tool for managers and their direct reports

In alignment with a corporate initiative to ensure practice of a growth mindset at the executive level, external coaches were maintained for most senior executives. In addition, the company offered coaching to the director-level and high-potential employees through Optify, a coach-scaling organization. This included a coaching platform that allowed them to pair the coach and client, track the coaching engagements, and provide a management training resource library. Furthermore, the internal coaching staff was expanded with the training and certification of five individuals in the Talent Development Team.

To ensure optimum benefit for potential coaching clients, the Talent Development Team agreed to review requests for coaching of each employee. In this way, employees could be paired with the appropriate modality of coaching—either external or internal.

For all people managers and their reports, Deltek leveraged an

AI-driven leadership coaching tool called LEADx. This technology provided tailored leadership competency learning material targeted to personalized areas of development. Algorithms formulated through behavioral assessments and articulated goals determine the content. For example, if a manager was identified as needing support on delegation, materials to read as well as daily messages or "nudges" would be sent to the manager on a behavior they might implement that day to enhance their delegation. Deltek also stated the intent to track the engagement results of that manager to see if there are improvements and to identify new areas of development.

Reflecting on the program, Hope shared, "I am excited that we have identified resources to meet the needs of every employee and support a culture of continuous learning and development through personalized coaching. There have been a lot of options for leadership training, but now we can expand the coaching to far more people in our company with the diverse coaching modalities that balance the different needs and cost limitations."

THE ORGANIZATION-TARGET COACHING PROGRAM IMPACT MODEL

This arrangement aligns the coaching strategy with the organization strategy in a holistic way. It is the most impactful and broad in scope because its deployment directly affects the success of important organizational change or challenges. Through this model, the coaching program is tailored to address the achievement of the desired organizational outcomes by developing the coaching strategy in tandem with the change or operational strategy. The CPS is instrumental in designing a program that may include different types, tools, and models of coaching in one initiative. And because of the high-level strategic impact of this model, the C-Suite leadership is engaged.

I see this model used in conjunction with mergers and acquisitions. For example, a company might acquire another company and then identify a desired organizational outcome to merge the operations with an aggressive timetable. The firm might identify the Human Challenge presented by this change and bring in a CPS to help create the coaching program. The CPS selects key audiences that will need coaching support to enhance their adoption of the change. The coaching program is created to enhance the process.

In addition, I frequently find this model implemented during a culture transformation. Since a culture transformation requires a change throughout the organization, using coaching to support the shift can have a speedier impact. In fact, many organizations now want to transform their organizations to a coaching culture that overall enhances change and growth.

> Since a culture transformation requires a change throughout the organization, using coaching to support the shift can have a speedier impact.

> "Our only security is our ability to change."
> —JOHN LILLY, NEUROSCIENTIST, PSYCHOANALYST, PHILOSOPHER, AND WRITER

Of particular note, when this type of model is used, other models may be used as well. For instance, the Organization-Target may serve as an umbrella, with Individual-Target and Audience-Target underneath, due to the complexity.

AN ORGANIZATION-TARGET COACHING PROGRAM MODEL EXAMPLE

A technology company recognized that it would become obsolete if it didn't reconfigure its business. To meet the challenge of a transformation, it raised funds by demutualizing and becoming a publicly traded company. As a result, the company had to meet shareholder expectations, which required double-digit revenue growth, as well as aggressive acquisitions of new businesses. This led to steep increase in employees, and its workforce grew substantially.

The CEO felt the primary barrier to transformation was having the right people on the executive team. He needed people who not only knew how to operate as a publicly traded company and help forge new business opportunities but also could lead differently. The CEO agreed with the board of directors to evaluate and "upskill" the leadership team as necessary to meet the company's objectives. Over the next two years, the company hired new executive team members with the right mix of skills and backgrounds.

Unfortunately, just replacing the people on the executive team didn't lead to the result the CEO had anticipated. The executive team was bogged down with low trust, along with territorial and contentious behavior. This tension permeated to other levels in the organization.

The CEO was confronted with the fact that transformation of the business surely couldn't happen without a unified and collaborative effort. This had to take place, not just in the executive team but also throughout the organization. Once he realized this, he understood that the company needed a cultural transformation. This would allow it to grow at pace into new business markets with new services and products.

The CEO worked with the CHRO and Cathy Manginelli, the chief talent officer, to create a culture change strategy. The strategy integrated coaching teams and individuals with leadership training. The CEO started first with the executive team. A three-pronged strategy was used for the executive team, which included team coaching, individual transition, and executive coaching. The executive team coaching consisted of weeklong dedicated team sessions once per quarter.

During these sessions, the team tackled their internal dynamics and identified new working norms and systems to hold each other mutually accountable. They found collaboration to be a key priority for the team and established metrics to track their success. The team also worked on building strategy and vision together. Each executive participated in building a mutually accountable business strategy.

In tandem with the team coaching, two types of individual coaching were deployed. Transition coaching assisted new executives to transition into the company. Executive coaching supported the executives in their own leadership development needs. It also helped them integrate the new collaboration work norms that had been established during the team meetings.

Once the executive team identified their norms, vision, and strategy and began their journey toward greater collaboration, they needed to cascade and permeate those same principles, behaviors, and ways of working to their teams. The organization had to scale the approach to coaching in a way that would accommodate many of their other leaders. To do so, the Talent Management team designed a strategic approach to embed coaching for the "next level of leader" into their leadership and management programs.

To progress in the leadership development curriculum from the baseline to advance courses, leaders were required to engage with a certified coach. The company considered coaching to be a critical element to one's leadership development journey. It supported and assisted them in the learning loop required to integrate these new competencies. In addition, the concept of coaching was reinforced through the performance management process as a key element to development planning and employee growth. Individual coaching engagements were evaluated with a review of 360 leadership profile measures, participation rates in leadership programs, behavior change, anecdotal feedback, and surveys.

To sustain the transformation, coaches were made available to all employees through a coach-scaling organization. This external coach provision service offered various types of coaching, such as mental health, sleep coach, and professional development. It also provided options such as long-term and "on-demand" type engagements.

The company worked with the coach-scaling organization to ensure they had tools, training materials, and insights, so the coaching cemented the learning designed by the HR department. As a result, the company achieved both their business growth goals and the cultural shift to a more collaborative and agile workplace.

As we consider coaching program impact models, the key concept is to think about outcomes first. We'll want to ask questions like, "What do we want the program to achieve?" After answering the question, we can design the need and choose the model. In addition, it's not essential to use only one model. As we've seen, some organizations may benefit from using more than one model to successfully carry out their organization's desired outcomes. In this sense, coaching can truly be customized to enhance individual, team, and organization performance.

CHAPTER SUMMARY: AT A GLANCE

- When using coaching to achieve desired organizational outcomes, it's important to recognize that every organization is unique. The specifics of the coaching program plan will reflect this.

- Impact models in coaching refer to the scope of the target for the coaching.

- Different impact models require different levels of program management and senior leadership involvement.

- The Individual-Target Coaching Program Impact Model centers on a single person's performance or a team's performance. This model is a common way to enhance performance of key individuals and teams within an organization, usually resulting in benefits for the organization beyond the individual or team.

- The Audience-Target Coaching Program Impact Model targets groups of individuals within a company and has a broader impact on multiple individuals, teams, or both. The targeting of a group of employees will address specific needs of that population to achieve organizational goals. This model requires somewhat more strategy building from leadership and coordination to execute.

- The Organization-Target Coaching Program Impact Model is used to help achieve overall desired organizational outcomes. It may include a mix of targets that has a holistic organization focus. Changing culture or company structure can often use this model of coaching. This model requires the most senior leadership involvement and oversight.

CHAPTER 10

Putting It in Action:
The Coaching Program Strategy

"When you connect with what you really want and why—and take action—magical things can happen."

—EMMA-LOUISE ELSEY, WRITER, COACH, AND ENTREPRENEUR

We have reviewed the techniques of powerful coaching and what aligns it to organizational outcomes and reviewed the diverse types, tools, and models of coaching that can be applied in organizations. Now, it is important to apply these elements in a strategic fashion to maximize the power of coaching for real, tangible, and long-lasting organizational outcomes.

In this chapter, I identify the key steps to design a coaching program. They encompass creating clarity of the overall organizational outcomes, diagnosing the potential human barriers to these outcomes, and then crafting the elements of an organizational coaching program strategy. I provide some examples where organizations have applied the steps in order to demonstrate how they work. Finally, I present an example of a petrol services business that developed a comprehensive coaching strategy to transform its business in a changing marketplace with an external Coach Program Strategist in "A Company Applies a Strategic Coaching Program to Transform Its Business."

STEP-BY-STEP: THE COACHING PROGRAM STRATEGY

The following steps of the process are meant to assist with thinking through the elements of a strategic coaching program. They include defining the bigger-picture objectives before designing the tactical elements. I'll spend the next sections going through each of these steps in more detail.

Best Practices for Strategic Coaching

1   Identify the Organization Challenge and Desired Organizational Outcome

2   Enlist the Coaching Program Strategist

3   Assess the Human Challenges Requiring Generative Learning

4   Create a Coaching Plan That Integrates Complementary Programs

5   Identify the Coaches

6   Prepare the Clients

7   Prepare the Coach Program

8 Review Policies and Create Coaching Contracts

9 Select the Coaching Tools

10 Provide Quality Control and Feedback

11 Measure Success and Outline Next Steps

1 IDENTIFY THE ORGANIZATION CHALLENGE AND DESIRED ORGANIZATIONAL OUTCOME

The "organization challenge" is the area of concern or the larger playing field where a change needs to occur. For instance, has the business seen a dip in sales or in productivity? Does the nonprofit need to change culture, or is it struggling with a culture clash within its ranks? Has the firm failed to keep pace with its competitors in innovating new products? Have market pressures caused a company to move from a high-profit-margin business to a commodity paradigm?

After the organization challenge has been identified, the desired organizational outcome is defined in a way that gives clarity to what success would look like. This involves stating what you wish to achieve. For example, in the case of a merger, the desired organizational outcome may be to expediently marry two organizations while retaining key talent. During this step, I always recommend creating a measurable, targeted organizational outcome. I've often heard organizational leaders express an aspiration to create more diversity. That's a valid aspiration; an organizational outcome, however, might be "to reduce attrition levels of a certain target group to a specific level within the next x years." This level of specificity allows the organization to be more exact when developing and unfolding the coaching program.

CASE ILLUSTRATION

An Organization's Diversity Initiatives

A professional services firm found it difficult to maintain diversity among higher levels of leadership. In particular, very few women had leading roles within the organization. These low numbers for female workers began at the senior manager level and dwindled further at the partner level.

Identifying the Organization Challenge

Upon closer inspection, it became clear that women in the firm faced several issues that needed to be addressed. These challenges were:

- A lack of focus on life balance to allow for time with family. Most men in the firm had traditional marriages where the wife cared for the family and the husband worked at the office. This created concerns that it was not possible to be a female partner while simultaneously having a family and being involved in a marriage in which both parents worked.

- Male bias against forming teams with women.

The Desired Organizational Outcome

After identifying the business challenge, the firm carried out research to explore ways to resolve its low diversity numbers. The desired organizational outcomes were to:

- Address the life balance and bias issues by educating the workforce as a whole and tracking women's involvement with top clients and projects.

- Meet a specific female partnership percentage goal in four years.

2 ENLIST THE COACHING PROGRAM STRATEGIST

An important step is to assign a CPS. This individual will lead the organization through both the setup and deployment of the coaching program. A CPS typically has organizational management expertise and program design competency. They understand the different models of coaching, along with how to best design and apply them.

The CPS may be internal to the company, often housed in Human Resources or Talent Development areas of the organization. Alternatively, the CPS may be an external consultant. Regardless of their origin, it is essential that the CPS work with the highest level of leadership within the organization overseeing the organizational outcome. By working with leaders, the CPS can ensure the coaching program is effectively tailored to lead to the organizational outcomes. A CPS is best served when they can design across various talent development platforms, such as training and mentoring programs, to dovetail them with the coaching program. They will oversee a portfolio of internal and external coaches, along with other coaching and training tools, to ensure program coherence.

> A CPS is best served when they can design across various talent development platforms, such as training and mentoring programs, to dovetail them with the coaching program.

CASE ILLUSTRATION

A CPS Steers a Company through Two Mergers

Philipia Hillman, the VP of Culture and Engagement at a defense contractor, needed to help her company undergo a merger and integrate with another company. In surveying the situation, she understood the biggest hurdle would be the Human Challenge of resentment. This typically builds as senior leaders explain the benefits and compatibility of merging, while the reality consists of constant and difficult renegotiating. Philipia knew there can often be a sense of bait and switch, as systems and processes are created and then recreated during the merger.

To help navigate the change, Philipia took on the CPS role. In her position, she could see that the best way to catalyze her people for change involved targeting managers just below the executive team. She wanted to provide them with coaching skills training. This training assisted the management cohort responsible for most of the change management. They were able to adopt and foster open mindsets and lead with curiosity rather than resentment.

A few years later, the company underwent another merger. At that time, the growth mindset leaders Philipia had helped develop during the previous merger tended to stay on. Rather than suffer, they thrived in the newly formed entity. Indeed, they had gained an ability to adjust to change. The wise CPS had used her knowledge of change management and coaching tools to help navigate two significant organizational changes.

3 ASSESS THE HUMAN CHALLENGES REQUIRING GENERATIVE LEARNING

Working through an organization change or asking employees to adopt new behaviors and competencies inevitably will present the Human Challenge as we described in chapter 3, which requires generative learning. These challenges can impact the ability of the organization to achieve desired outcomes. Articulating these Human Challenges can help the CPS design the right coaching program to mitigate the pushback and leverage the energy to change.

"Slowness to change usually means fear of the new."
—PHILIP CROSBY, BUSINESSMAN AND AUTHOR

To articulate the challenges, I suggest asking the following:

- Who is impacted in this change to achieve an organizational outcome?

- What behaviors and competencies must they develop?

- What fears may arise? For example, will there be threats to a sense of competency, job, or other types of security loss? Will there be a change in the ability to control or influence their environment? Might they feel professional and personal relationship threats and loss?

- What shifts in institutional or individual values are required to meet this organizational outcome?

- What mindsets will need to be different during the change?

- What must we do to support our people through this change?

This exercise helps an organization to identify coaching outcomes that can be tracked to measure success. Suppose a nonprofit would like to have a more collaborative culture. I might ask, "What behaviors of which people do we want to see that would tell us we are more collaborative?" Or I may inquire, "What competencies do we want to see with leaders who are collaborative?"

In addition to these questions, formal research may be used to assess barriers and needed competencies, including surveys of the affected populations. The surveys can pose questions about what employees expect to be their biggest challenges in the change. Focus groups or one-on-one conversations with leaders and staff can identify certain areas that are harder to assess in surveys. When working with higher-level leaders, these interviews can produce a more refined sense of what they fear for themselves and their people.

Alternatively, an organization's leadership may choose to forego the formal research. Instead, they might opt to hold brainstorming sessions with a diverse set of leaders. These leaders can weigh in and posit what they believe are the biggest barriers to change for the given circumstance.

CASE ILLUSTRATION

A Pharmaceutical Company Faces an Adaptive Challenge Requiring Generative Learning

A pharmaceutical company had gaps in their succession plan. The firm wanted to build young leaders earlier in their careers, so the leader pool would be deeper. To do so, they hired only the best scientific talent.

While this grounded their scientific expertise, they lacked the leadership skills to manage talent and provide strong leaders for their growing business. The first approach to solving the problem was technical in nature. They changed the internal review system with senior leader feedback to their reports from a system of twice per year tied to promotion and compensation to a just-in-time feedback system where leaders critiqued reports' performance more continuously.

Unfortunately, under this strategy, senior leaders delivered feedback perhaps in alignment with their scientific training without applying an understanding of the emotional intelligence skills needed to deliver the feedback effectively. Technical leaders struggled to understand a mindset of growth through critical feedback. Their training in science was focused on technical accuracy and quality. When they encountered issues with their employees, they branded them as faulty or wrong. This led to a high attrition rate.

The CEO realized that a simple technical solution—changing the personnel review system—was not enough to develop future leaders. The culture change was to move senior leadership mindsets from critical evaluation to supportive coach-like feedback focused on growth of the junior leader rather than criticism. That was a generative change that required both training and coaching. The CEO and HR department worked together to hire a CPS to help them design the coaching plan. The coaching program included both coaching skills training and coaching one-on-one for the executive team. The coaching skills training was a two-day program that taught coaching skills to roughly five hundred managers and executives, including the executive team. The training was interactive to help leaders understand the impact of inquiry and listening and help them create not just coaching skills but a coaching and growth mindset.

Importantly, the twelve-member executive team was coached one-on-one for a year to ensure integration of both the coaching skills and the coaching mindset. It was essential for the executive team to most profoundly adopt a shift in values around how to think about feedback as a positive growth experience instead of an evaluation process.

This change in the executive team's mindset, as well as engaging in a learning loop of practice, led to a successful result. Junior leaders were coached by senior leaders to build their ability to take on higher levels of management, and the attrition numbers declined.

4 CREATE A COACHING PLAN THAT INTEGRATES COMPLEMENTARY PROGRAMS

The coaching plan articulates the strategy and process for the coaching engagement. The strategy includes the statement of the organization challenges, Human Challenges, and desired organizational outcomes. The coaching process outlines how individual and team coaches will be selected and deployed and dovetail with any other programs. It lists the time line for the rollout of the various stages of the program. It covers quality control touch points, any measurement tools, and coach and client feedback. A sample coaching program plan follows.

COACHING PROGRAM PLAN

(One-Page Overview)

Organization Challenge

We are transforming our product mix to include software products and services that support our audit services. It is currently December, and we are planning to transform during the coming year. There is internal resistance to the adoption of the new technologies and sluggish sales.

Desired Organizational Outcome

For the partners to adopt and sell in the new technology service model by June of next year.

Associated Behaviors and Competencies

Partners will work effectively with software engineers to tailor customer solutions as well as sell in standard products. They will focus on respect for the engineer role, how to communicate with the technical expert, and how to tackle your biases.

Engineers will master communication skills, including inquiry and listening.

Human Challenges

Our inquiry found the biggest challenge would be concerns of competency for senior partners regarding the switch to technology-based products they don't understand and will need to sell. Part of this can be addressed by more knowledge, but part will be addressed by a closer partnership with, and respect for, our engineering staff. There are feelings of loss of control or "supremacy" that inhibit this collaboration. The engineers also lack fluency in customer-facing skills and need to develop better customer-focused communication.

Coaches

Internal and external coaches. A group of four internal and four external coaches will coach twenty senior partners and twenty engineers.

Time Line

- Coaching for six months

- In January, a three-hour training program by Talent Development personnel: Sales and Communication and Bias Training for Partners, and a three-hour training by Talent Development personnel: Communication and Customer Focus

Materials and Complementary Programs

- Go to market sales training and support materials

- Program objectives memo with specified process changes

- Training pieces with "How to Collaborate" pointers

- Coaching agreements

Program Preparation

On January 1, coaches and clients will meet with leadership for the video program launch to discuss expectations and introduce materials. Coaches and clients will all be versed in the online progress tracking and quality reporting tool.

Coaching Alignment and Evaluation

- Alignment meetings will occur with partner and leader, and engineer and leader in January, and again after the completion of six coaching sessions.

- Quality survey by coaches and clients will be carried out on March 15 and at program completion.

- HR business partner will conduct survey of leaders of engineers and partners to evaluate program success.

- Sales revenues will be tracked for twelve months with a six-month review with HR partner around behavior goal pulse assessment.

IDENTIFY THE COACHES

When implementing coaching, an organization decides how to source the coaches. The organization may decide to develop a staff of internal coaches or hire external coaches. There are some distinct benefits to internal coaches, but there are also drawbacks to be aware of when deploying them.

Defining an Internal Coach

An internal coach is defined as a coach who is employed by the company and coaches other employees of the company through a formal coaching relationship. Some organizations, such as SAP (described in chapter 1), may certify employees in coaching and allow them to coach up to a certain percentage of their job time. Internal coaches use the coaching process, including contracting with their clients, with coaching goals and working toward actions that engage the client in a learning loop. The certified training and structured approach ensure the coaching is clearly distinguished from other types of activities like mentoring or consulting.

A clear distinction should be made between other types of leadership support, such as advising or mentorship and training programs. If the term "coaching" is used, then the relationship is built to empower the client and to build a learning mindset, not to receive consulting or advising. The coaching relationship can dovetail with the integration of training but is not simply a transfer of information.

Some individuals such as HR professionals may have one-off conversations with a client to help them brainstorm a problem or navigate a political situation. These are more effectively termed "advisory sessions," as they usually entail a problem-focused approach that ends with the problem and solution defined. Often the internal resource is sharing knowledge or information that helps the client solve their problem, and this is closer to consulting or advising than coaching.

Confidentiality

The coaching relationship is founded on confidentiality, as coaching requires deep trust for the client to bring forward meaningful and difficult issues. The potential for confidentiality to be compromised or even perceived to be compromised creates problems for the internal coach. For example, imagine a coach who works in a Human Resources department. They may promise complete confidentiality of any conversation. However, what happens if, during the course of the job, they are asked to provide input on succession or promotions that involve their current or former client?

> *The coaching relationship is founded on confidentiality, as coaching requires deep trust for the client to bring forward meaningful and difficult issues.*

As a point of reference, The International Coaching Federation provides guidelines for confidentiality and internal coaching. For internal coaches, it includes the following perspective:

> *When working as an Internal Coach, manage conflicts of interest or potential conflicts of interest with my coaching Clients and Sponsor(s) through coaching agreement(s) and ongoing dialogue. This should include addressing organizational roles, responsibilities, relationships, records, confidentiality, and other reporting requirements.*[13]

Another challenge to confidentiality arises when an internal coach is interacting and coaching with multiple people throughout an organization. The internal coach needs to ensure that knowledge about one client doesn't get shared with another client. While the sharing of information seems easy to control, there are subtle nuances that coaches learn about a client that may come forward in conversation. Strong awareness is required to manage confidentiality in these settings and not reveal clues or private information.

Cost

The cost of external coaches is often clearer than the cost of internal coaches. External coaches work on a contract and do not require benefits or overhead and use minimal internal resources. Internal coaches are often perceived to be cheaper than external coaches. However, internal coaches require all the benefits of regular employees and, therefore, may carry greater cost than an external coach. And if the organization goes through a financial downturn, it is much harder to terminate an internal coach than to terminate a contract with an external coach.

Expertise

It is essential to evaluate the certifications of coaches before selecting them. The International Coaching Federation is one of the top international certifying organizations and has competency standards for three levels of coaches. These levels are: Associate Certified Coach (ACC), Professional Certified Coach (PCC), and Master Certified Coach (MCC). Higher-level certifications indicate more hours of experience and a higher standard of quality of coaching. The International Coaching Federation also has a referral service that lists all coaches, their geography, and their certification levels. For internal coaches, the program manager should ensure the proper certification and skills are achieved and address where their coaches need more training. If team coaching will be used, it will be important to look for coaches who are proficient at team optimization and development coaching.

In general, external coaches have deeper coaching expertise in the sense that they see many different leaders across different industries and sectors. This gives them the kind of broad leadership expertise we typically see in consultants. External coaches invest in their continued development as coaches and will often be part of a broader coaching community or certification organization that requires continued education and promotes conferences and workshops that assist coaches in the continued development of their expertise.

Internal coaches, on the other hand, may be focused on other activities. They might carry other roles as a part-time coach, or they may manage human resources or talent development programs. These activities may divert their attention to other areas. As a result, they could be distracted from a sole focus on coaching.

Still, internal coaches often know the culture and players of the organization in which they are an employee better than external coaches. They understand the various political powers at play or know to what norms the clients are subject. If an internal coach is careful not to fall prey to biases, this can be a strong advantage. This is particularly the case when coaches are deployed against a change initiative in which political intricacies can be at play.

Bias and the Hidden Agenda

In general, coaches are taught to be aware of their personal biases when coaching a client. As an employee of an organization, we often have strong opinions on what direction the company should go, on which leaders we prefer, what we want people to do for us or our division, and so on. An internal coach must separate themselves from these preferences or bias when coaching. They must be willing to hear plans that an executive may share with them that might lead to cuts in their division or less desirable outcomes for their people. In my coach training, I often say, "Don't coach your family and friends." We are often heavily vested in the outcomes of the coaching of people who share our lives. With acquaintances and loved ones, it is too hard to remain impartial.

Client "Power"

The client and the coach are partners in the client coaching experience. Unlike therapy or mentoring, coaching presumes equal power on the part of client and coach. The expertise of the coach is to help the client define their goals and create an environment of deep curiosity in which the client can explore how to arrive at the goals. The coach also helps the client define actions that will get them to these goals and to integrate the learning from the actions. The coach does not solve the problem or profess to have the right answers.

For the internal coach, this can be a challenge due to their intimate knowledge of the organization's operations. The internal coach can share knowledge, as long as it is clear that the knowledge is public information and not personal perception. They can share a best practice, idea, or resource. The sharing must always be couched in the neutral territory that allows the client to accept or reject it.

Organizations often follow a common practice of having senior leaders choose external coaches rather than internal coaches. This may be due to issues of confidentiality or can stem from the complications of positional power over the coach and/or the coaching operation.

CASE ILLUSTRATION

Selecting Internal and External Coaches

Alejandro leads the Human Resources department in Mexico for a division of a multinational auto products firm. His division works primarily on research and development and is composed of roughly 1,600 engineers and staff. In the early 2000s, he moved from being a full-time engineer into the HR role and started to train as a coach.

At that time, he deployed coaching with a small team of individuals to assist employees with Six Sigma and Lean Manufacturing. The coaching was used more as an application of coaching skills than a formal structured form of coaching. As he continued to see the benefits of coaching, he decided to build a coaching program including external and internal coaches and coach skills training for managers and leaders. The external coaches were used to coach the executive staff on a request basis. For the internal coaches, he selected a group of employees to take formal coach training and then deployed them as part-time coaches. To complement the individual coaching relationships, he integrated coach skills training into the Leadership Training Program including listening, powerful questions, and the "Ask, don't tell" approach.

In one powerful application of the coaching, Alejandro trained and deployed fifteen internal coaches to run a career coaching program that helped the participants take greater control over their careers and to think more proactively about their choices. One of the aspects of coaching highly appreciated by the engineering talent was the coaching structure—goal identification, current state assessment, scenario development and next steps planning—and the ability of the coaches to build the clients' sense of empowerment and ownership of their careers. The coaching team coached over 150 participants and saw over 80 percent of them find new positions within the company within five years. This assisted in high retention and engagement rates for the company. Many of the participants listed their sense of being listened to and invested in as key factors to their job satisfaction.

For more on deploying internal coaches go to linktr.ee/sandrastewart.com.

6   PREPARE THE CLIENTS

A common problem when engaging a coach stems from a lack of client preparation. All too often coaches are assigned to clients, and the client does not have a context for the coaching. In these cases, clients are left to wonder if the coaching was assigned because something was "wrong" with their behavior. This, of course, can carry negative connotations.

For this reason, I strongly advise communicating the mission of the overall coaching program. It's important to tell the client why they were chosen to participate in the program before they meet the coach. Organizations can also educate potential clients about the topic of coaching. They might provide written or intranet-based materials that discuss what coaching is and how it is different from other programs such as training, mentoring, and consulting. The documents should share policies regarding who is awarded coaching in the organizations, along with the purposes and expected outcomes.

When this initial legwork is done, the coach and client are able to begin the coaching with clarity. There is an understanding about any organizational or leader expectations from the coaching. Alignment meetings (covered in chapter 8) are important as a next step to begin the conversation between leader and client to enhance organizational alignment.

 7 PREPARE THE COACH PROGRAM

Preparing coaches to engage with clients is important for gaining consistency across a diverse portfolio of coaches. The coach preparation might include one or more meetings before the program launch. In these meetings, the objectives for the coaching are shared so coaches comprehend their role in the project and the project goals. The individual managing the logistics of the coaching program, often referred to as the coaching program coordinator, will be heavily involved in these meetings. The coaching program coordinator will provide information that is relevant to the program on organization culture, structure, key leaders, and—importantly—organization and leader expectations. The coaching cohort may also have a meeting with the executive leaders to have the opportunity to ask questions and gain the confidence of the organization. If any coaching tools are to be used in the coaching engagement, the coaches may need training on the tools and a common understanding of what the expected outcomes of the tools will be for their clients.

Having support from the coaching program coordinator for the coaches and organization leaders is key throughout the program. This is particularly helpful if problems arise. If a coach finds that the client is not attending their coaching meetings, or is not benefitting from the coaching, and conversations with the client don't rectify the situation, they can turn to the coaching program coordinator to address the situation. The coaching program coordinator can speak to the client and determine if another coach is needed, or if the client is not in a position to accept coaching at that time.

A coaching program coordinator and CPS of multiple coaching engagements may organize coach cohort meetings, which allow the coaches to communicate general trends that don't violate confidentiality. They may share resources that have come to light during the coaching that advance best practices across the coach cohort. The approach can help identify possible roadblocks to the desired organizational outcome that the leadership did not anticipate. The CPS can then share these possible roadblocks, and the program can be tweaked.

Using technology platforms (which are outlined in chapter 8) can enhance the process of preparing clients and coaches. Some companies develop an internal technology platform, while others license a coach-scaling platform such as Optify for this step. Through these platforms, the organizations can pair coaches and clients and create a shared space for material. The platform can be used to distribute documents about the program objective, along with educational information and contracts for the program.

8   REVIEW POLICIES AND CREATE COACHING CONTRACTS

Contracts are important for the success of the coaching engagement to create clarity in the coaching relationship. They outline confidentiality and logistics issues as well as the responsibilities of the coach, client, and sponsor.

As a profession, coaching requires a strong ethical practice to maintain trust between the coach and the organization, between the coach and the client, and between the client and the organization. For this reason, it's essential to be clear about expectations for all parties involved. Contracts help provide this clarity for everyone. Here is a breakdown of common contracts that can be used and how they work:

- *Coach and Organization Contract*: This type of contract specifies confidentiality limitations and program deliverables on the part of both the coach and the organization. Deliverables might include what assessments the coach or organization will provide, the quality processes that will be deployed, and the forms of communication required by the coach with the organization or CPS. If the coach is external to the organization, a nondisclosure agreement is often included. In addition, any insurance or liability matters are addressed.

- *Coach and Client Contract*: This contract serves to create transparency. It ensures confidentiality and states policies and procedures. If the coach will be communicating engagement of the client back to the organization, that should be clear to the client.

- *Organization and Client Contract*: This document helps communicate the expectations that the organization has from the coaching program. The organization should clearly communicate the scope of the coaching and what they hope to achieve by it. If the communication is that the coaching is fully for the benefit of the client, then the client will know there is a wide latitude on which the coaching can be focused. If the communication indicates the coaching is to achieve specific competencies or adopt systems, then those expectations should be clear to the client as a foundation for the coaching. This contracting can be conducted formally in writing or through alignment meetings with the coach, client, organization supervisor, or HR leader.

9 SELECT THE COACHING TOOLS

Coaching tools are generally designed and tailored to fit the goals of the coaching program. They may include curriculum, articles, podcasts, books, consulting models, frameworks, technical tools, or instructional media. (In chapter 8, I discuss technologies that may be used in conjunction with coaching to create learning and training programs as well as habit and behavior change tracking.) These are developed or selected by the coach program manager collaborating with leadership.

Assessments are another tool used in coaching programs. Leadership competencies, work and communication style, and motivations might all be assessed and shared across levels of leadership. Once again, the shared applications of the assessments help an organization create continuity across leader groups or organization areas.

10 PROVIDE QUALITY CONTROL AND FEEDBACK

A strong coaching program should include quality feedback systems for the quality of performance of coaches. I have found that both coaches and clients generally benefit from a midpoint survey. A simple survey can assess if the coach is meeting the needs of the client. It can also determine if the client is familiar with the coaching tools or frameworks that were a part of the coaching objectives. In addition, this survey allows an opportunity for the client to reflect more deeply. The midpoint feedback can be shared with the coach, who can then implement more helpful coaching behaviors. After the coaching term is completed, another quality assessment can determine the overall coach performance. The coaching program coordinator can use this to assess if the coach needs further development for future projects.

Client engagement is the job of both the client and coach. If the client is not engaged in the coaching, the issue must be quickly addressed to maintain the value of the investment. Engagement can be assessed by a third party surveying the client's satisfaction with the coaching. The coach may also flag a client that is not engaging well in the sessions, cancelling, or not showing up for meetings. The supervisor can use alignment meetings to flag if the client seems disengaged. The client and coach relationship should incorporate check-ins on how the coaching is going for the client, so the coach can reset with any direct feedback.

11 MEASURE SUCCESS AND OUTLINE NEXT STEPS

At the beginning of the program launch, the leadership and the CPS will determine success metrics for the coaching program. Surveys, interviews, and focus groups can serve to measure these metrics during and after the program. For example, if the desired organizational outcome is to catalyze leaders' ability to develop their reports, the coaching program can measure if yearly reviews have been completed. The program can provide surveys to direct reports that evaluate to what extent they perceive their leader to support their development. The program can also audit the level of promotions achieved by the people of different leaders. If the organization goal is to retain diversity in their ranks, a survey to the clients can determine what impact the coaching program has had on their desire to stay with the firm. Alternatively, coaching could be offered to some populations and not others so that attrition can be compared between the two groups.

There are many ways to measure ROI and success in coaching programs. A good amount of research has been carried out in these areas. You can access the research and more information on measuring coaching success through organizations such as the International Coaching Federation.

In sum, while these eleven steps can be valuable for an organization that wants to deploy strategic coaching to achieve organizational outcomes, I also encourage them to be used as food for thought. In other words, implementing these steps can take place in various forms with different time lines. In my experience, the organizations that reap the most benefits from these practices are those that customize them to fit their precise culture, structure, and unique needs. When that's done, the true magic of coaching can unfold.

CASE ILLUSTRATION

A Company Applies a Strategic Coaching Program to Transform Its Business

A gas services company in Slovenia identified their organization challenge as existential. They were faced with market pressure to move from petroleum products and services toward green energy sources. If they didn't act proactively and transform their business, other energy sources in the industry would undercut their revenue.

The company recognized that they would need to create an agile company culture to bring them through this transition. Leadership developed these **desired organizational outcomes**:

- A leadership behavior change from telling to empowering
- An employee mindset shift from "change is bad" to a growth mindset
- Innovation leaders requiring a competency change from managing an established business to leading growing businesses that could adjust to industry change
- A culture change from passive to innovative

To execute this business transformation, the company brought in Tatjana Dragovic Andersen as the **CPS**. Tatjana worked with leadership to identify and design a program to address the Human Challenges in mindsets and readiness for change. Most importantly, she laid out a business-wide solution that would embed a sustainable mindset change so that culture change would last. Tatjana built a **coaching program plan** that integrated training with individual, team, and group coaching.

Tatjana worked to align the coaching strategy to fully achieve innovation and a growth mindset for the company by first **identifying coaches** and **preparing the clients** for the **coaching program**. The program focused initially on executive team training around innovation and growth mindset. The training was paired with individual coaching sessions to integrate the training. In addition to the innovation and growth mindset training, the coaching program would train executives on coaching skills so that they could support their managers' growth. These coaching skills helped leaders build the ability to empower others to think creatively and grow.

The training occurred semimonthly with individual coaching in between training sessions. After launching the executive team effort, the middle management teams were brought on board with similar trainings paired with coaching. These trainings were half as frequent with the assumption that executive leadership would be able to help integrate the new learnings with their managers with their newly developed coaching skills. Finally, the staff-level trainings were similar but conducted as group training and coaching sessions.

Another impactful part of the program focused on building coaching and training competencies inside the HR department to ensure ongoing support of the new leader and manager mindsets and competencies. By building internal training and coaching competencies, the changes being implemented had greater sustainability.

Throughout the program Tatjana oversaw **quality control and feedback** to ensure the coaching program stayed on track. She helped monitor the most important coaching objectives with specific metrics. To do this, she used the TOMS (Topic, Objective, Measures, Success). One Topic, or focus on change, was to shift teams to include more diverse decision-making. Objectives were built around the types of meetings and the process by which diverse views were incorporated. Measures were established to determine success on these objectives, such as a trained observer sitting in on meetings to assess frequency and the type of meeting contributions and selection of agenda items. Success was determined on a rated scale by the observer, so they could demonstrate how well each team was able to implement the objectives and then act on the feedback to modify their behaviors.

The coaching program lasted three years. The final year provided some unique opportunities to create communication and understanding up and down the organization. This was a group coaching program. Several mixed-level groups of diverse participants including staff, middle management, and leaders continued the coach-facilitated conversations to embed the culture change. This also enhanced the leaders' appreciation of the talent that existed throughout the organization and helped them to better understand the impact of the changes on the business.

In today's world, organizations must evolve quickly to navigate changes. Employees need to pivot quickly, take on new roles, and work in different ways. Deploying coaches can catalyze the ability of a workforce to adopt the core competencies of change including new skill sets, learning to deal with uncertainty and change, and breaking down fear-based decision-making or avoidance. Organizations that think through their challenges, lay out their desired organizational outcomes, and develop a plan to carry out will be able to use coaching strategically to truly reap success.

CHAPTER SUMMARY: AT A GLANCE

- Regardless of the scope of the coaching program, all applications of coaching benefit from a strategic and planful approach. This allows an organization to maximize value from the coaching.

- The best practices for successfully carrying out strategic coaching include the following steps: identify the organization challenge and organizational outcome, enlist the CPS, assess the Human Challenges and the generative changes, create a coaching plan, identify the coaches, prepare the clients, prepare the coach program, review policies and create coaching contracts, select the coaching tools, provide quality control and feedback, measure success, and outline next steps.

CHAPTER 11

Looking into the Future

"If one is lucky, a solitary fantasy can totally transform one million realities."
—MAYA ANGELOU

The power of coaching comes from its ability to enhance the capacity of people to learn, grow, and thrive in change. It is an essential tool in optimizing not just organizations, but also society as a whole. As I look to the future, I see how coaching will continue to integrate into the processes, products, and cultures of organizations. And when coaching is focused on societal ills, I see how it can accelerate the work of societal change.

In the following sections, we'll look at how coaching is being integrated into products and services, and where there are opportunities for more to be done in this area. We'll revisit the core competencies of change and review how coaching has helped organizations thrive in change. We'll also consider coaching initiatives that are transforming the quality of life in societies around the world.

INTEGRATING COACHING INTO PRODUCTS AND SERVICES

Coaching is now being integrated into the products and services of organizations. By pairing coaching services with the base product or service of a company, it shifts the mindset of the client from seeing the company as a seller to seeing them as a partner in success of a desired change in their business. This move—from product sales to partnership—will strengthen the loyalty of customer and product and service provider. The bond provides both a competitive advantage and a method to retain customers and clients.

To help us visualize this, we'll revisit the graphic we first viewed at the beginning of the book.

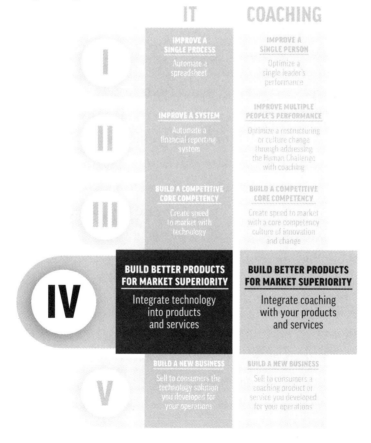

In the last two stages of integrating the core competencies of coaching, we see the opportunity to integrate coaching into current products and services and then potentially to build a market for these services direct to customers and consumers. The opportunities presented by using coaching and coaching skills to build out service offerings into different businesses are limitless. In the following examples, we'll see a few ways this is currently being carried out.

Consulting Firms

The reason to integrate coaching with consulting became clear during my consulting days. As a consultant, I would research the root causes of business challenges, write up and present an analysis, and share recommendations for action. The issue of adopting and implementing the recommendations remained with the client executive.

Under this arrangement, the executive was left with their own fears and concerns about the needed change. Moreover, once they announced the changes, they were confronted with the Human Challenge often in the form of resistance to change. At this point, the executive most needed support to plan for the needed changes. This lack of support could be why so many consulting recommendations are never realized.

In a different scenario, after the consultant delivers the recommendations, a Coaching Program Strategist is provided. This CPS is not vested in the executive adopting the consultant recommendations. Rather, the CPS is vested in the executive getting the support they need to do the reflecting and planning to make change. The coach and executive reflect on the needed change, understand the executive team's readiness, and then build a strategic coaching program for change.

While the coach is included in the contract provided by the consulting firm, they must have independence from the consultant's views and recommendations. This ensures the leader is given the control of the synthesis of the consultant's recommendations, so they can pick and choose what works for them and their organization. The coach's job is to help them integrate the learning from the consultant study, and then to reset the plan according to what they believe will work for them and their organization. The CPS assists the executive to build the coaching program to implement the change.

There are a number of consulting firms today that support organizational change execution. They have coaches that help the executive as well as the implementation teams. These consultancies lead with the consulting project and then design the coaching support on the back end.

Another type of firm starts with the coaching expertise rather than the organizational expertise. The Coach-Scaling Organization (see chapter 8) has a staff of vetted coaches. The CSO will work with the client organization to determine their change goals and then build a coaching program plan that helps the client achieve these strategic change goals.

Technology Firms

Technology companies, including service and product providers, provide products that are often rolled out to hundreds of end users in an organization. Training may be provided in the beginning of the implementation, but then the relationship is passed off to the customer service department. Often, individuals struggle with the human challenges presented in sustainably integrating new behaviors required for technology adoption.

If the technology company paired coaching services with their implementation, there is a higher likelihood of success of the technology adoption. Coaching could include a focus on leaders, teams, and groups of employees. Coaching leaders would include how best to communicate technology changes as well as how to adopt their own behavior changes. Team coaching could assist cross-functional teams where new communication systems and behaviors are required. Group coaching and peer coaching involving technology adoption could engage larger numbers of employees to share their concerns in the learning process that is required in integrating new technology.

If the technology company paired coaching services with their implementation, there is a higher likelihood of success of the technology adoption.

Communications Firms

Communication firms advise and help build communication strategies, programs, and internal systems for their clients. The success of these programs, like with consulting firms, depends upon the client's ability to adopt the systems including new processes or new technologies.

A communication firm could deploy a Coaching Program Strategist who would work with the client leaders overseeing the communication changes. Together, they could develop a coaching plan to integrate new strategies into their workplace that support employees through the adoption of new behaviors and mindsets.

Recruiting Firms

As discussed in chapter 1, recruiting firms assist organizations in hiring executives. Because of the expense to the client if the new hire fails, the recruiting firms are vested in the success of that executive's onboarding and retention. By using coaching programs to support that executive in their initial year on the job, recruiting firms can enhance the chances of success for the executive. Doing so can strengthen the loyalty of the client firm, which ultimately avoids the expense of a failed hire.

COACHING AND ORGANIZATIONAL COMPETENCIES OF CHANGE

As we observed in previous chapters, coaching is being used to create organizational cultures that can more effectively meet change. Coaching builds the core competencies of change, which we discussed in chapters 1 and 4. As a review, these basic core competencies are:

THE OPEN MIND
The ability to adopt new information and ideas

THE VALUES-DRIVEN SPIRIT
The ability to align with purpose consistent with one's values

THE CURIOUS MIND
The ability to challenge assumptions and the status quo and ask powerful questions

CORE COMPETENCIES OF CHANGE

THE OTHER-AWARE MIND
The ability to understand others

THE OPTIMISTIC MIND
The ability to think in terms of possibility and overcome hopelessness

THE SELF-AWARE MIND
The ability to explore and understand the self to better manage one's choices and impact on others

- The Open Mind—the ability to adopt new information and ideas

- The Curious Mind—the ability to challenge assumptions and the status quo and ask powerful questions

- The Optimistic Mind—the ability to think in terms of possibility and overcome hopelessness

- The Self-Aware Mind—the ability to explore and understand the self to better manage one's choices and impact on others

- The Other-Aware Mind—the ability to understand others

- The Values-Driven Spirit—the ability to align with purpose consistent with one's values

Throughout the book, I've shared real-life examples of how the core competencies of change have made a difference for organizations. Here is a quick listing of these examples; I encourage you to review those that might be of particular benefit to your situation or organization:

- *SAP Catalyzes Culture Change with Coaching* (p. 28)—in this case, a pioneering company in technology uses coaching to build a culture shift, grow new leadership skills, and enhance a talent development program.

- *A Pharmaceutical Company Faces an Adaptive Change Requiring Generative Learning* (p. 62 and p. 202)—this story relates how a company recognized the need for a generative learning culture in talent development.

- *An Organization Changes Its Culture by Building Growth Mindsets* (p. 69)—this story explains how a large healthcare system transformed its culture with the help of a strategic coaching program.

- *Coaching Teams to Transition to New Leadership* (p. 151)—this example shows how coaching with teams enhanced the ability to change through new leadership.

- *An Audience-Target Coaching Program Model Example* (p. 186)—this case details how a technology company targeted leaders to build growth mindsets.

- *An Organization-Target Coaching Program Model Example* (p. 190)—this case study depicts a global software and solutions company that built employees with growth mindsets.

- *A CPS Steers a Company through Two Mergers* (p. 200)—this story shows how core change competencies created executives who thrived in a merger and acquisition.

- *A Company Applies a Strategic Coaching Program to Transform Its Business* (p. 219)—this case study revealed a gas services company that transformed their culture to meet disruptive change.

COACHING AND SOCIETAL CHANGE

The world faces existential threats including environmental degradation on a global scale, inequities in wealth, and uneven access to resources and healthy livelihoods. For many of us, these problems are far too overwhelming to think that "I" can make a difference. These changes engender the most profound fear and insecurity, as well as ethical dilemmas.

Fixed mindsets that appear when we are threatened often come from a place of fear. We fear for our traditions, our livelihoods, and our familiar people, places, and values. We fear what we don't know. Coaching can assist our society in examining our fears and building the ability to take steps toward greater understanding of ourselves and others and to find the power of optimism and creative possibility.

Because coaching shifts people from fixed mindsets to growth mindsets and can uncover assumptions that impede change, it holds the possibility to help us navigate through the anxiety of existential threats. And because coaching helps us align with our values, find solutions, and build understanding of others, it can empower us to work together to build a better world.

We have proof that a small group of people can make a global difference using coaching. The International Coaching Federation Foundation is doing just that. The foundation's mission is to "Connect and equip professional coaches and organizations to accelerate and amplify impact on social progress through coaching." Under the ICF Foundation Strategic Impact Framework,[14] it established the Ignite program, which harnesses the global network of ICF coaches, including 140 chapters in seventy-five countries, to provide coaching toward strategic social change goals.

To focus its efforts, the Ignite program selected the United Nations Sustainable Development Goals to guide the deployment of the ICF chapters' resources.[15] According to the UN:

The Sustainable Development Goals are the blueprint to achieve a better and more sustainable future for all. They address the global challenges we face, including poverty, inequality, climate change, environmental degradation, peace, and justice.[16]

To begin the launch of the Ignite program, they chose to focus on the goal of education that states the following:

Education enables upward socioeconomic mobility and is a key to escaping poverty. Over the past decade, major progress was made towards increasing access to education and school enrollment rates

at all levels, particularly for girls. Nevertheless, about 260 million
children were still out of school in 2018—nearly one-fifth of the
global population in that age group. And more than half of all
children and adolescents worldwide are not meeting minimum
proficiency standards in reading and mathematics.[17]

The ICF Foundation tapped the talents and interests of their 140 chapters. They asked for chapters to reach out to educational organizations to gauge their interest in pro bono coaching for their leadership. Then the ICF Foundation provided chapters with support materials for onboarding and leading mass volunteer, pro bono coaching for these organizations.

According to Janet Harvey, former President of ICF Global, when the idea was first presented to chapters, it was expected that a handful might participate. In fact, 46 of the 140 chapters engaged. This remarkable response led to eighty educational organizations and 410 education leaders receiving coaching in North and South America, Asia, Europe, and Middle and East Africa. This overwhelming volunteer effort from a community of coaches made a real difference in the lives of people every day. In fact, these **eighty organizations now impact 16 million lives.**[18]

Leaders reported benefits in enhanced leadership, teamwork, and personal development and increased operational efficiency and workplace engagement that translated to a higher rate of performance in achieving their missions on all levels.

"Changing the world, one conversation at a time."
—TEODORA SKAMENOVA, IGNITE PROGRAM COACH[19]

IMPACT OF THE IGNITE PROGRAM

The Ignite program has led to an outpouring of stories around the world. These reflect gratitude from those who received coaching, anecdotes of personal and organizational transformation, and an optimistic view of the future. Here are only a few of these tales from the eighty organizations that received coaching in different corners of the world:

In Oman, the Ignite Program Project Manager Benita Stafford-Smith and Project Director Dr. Katy Bendon share that "this culture doesn't understand failure as a mechanism to problem-solving." They note the benefits of coaching has created a better culture for change by providing a sounding board to synthesize learnings and enhance leadership of key educational initiatives.[20]

In Bulgaria, the ICF chapter deployed coaches with six educational institution partners. Teodora Skamenova, a project manager, shared that one of the organizations was undergoing an organizational change. Through the coaching, the leaders were better prepared to manage through the complexities of change. She also found that the coaches were reconnected to a sense of purpose and energized as coaches.[21]

Ignite Program Coach Neil Camacho worked with a University in Costa Rica. He found that the university clients were amazed by the difference coaching made, not only in finding new tools and ideas professionally but also in achieving personal life goals. One of his clients shared, "It changed my life. I realize now that even though I had been well trained and had a postgraduate degree, I did not understand how to manage people."[22]

WHAT'S NEXT FOR COACHING

We've spent time in the previous sections and chapters outlining what coaching can do and how to align it with organizational strategy and outcomes. The outdated coaching approach of "coaching the problematic executive" is now long in the past, and we can look ahead with a more insightful view. We've seen how coaching has grown and evolved over the last several decades and how it is currently positioned to fit into an organization's processes and culture.

As we've also learned, using the right tools, methods, and planning is essential when incorporating coaching programs into an organization. Working with individuals who know the various tools, types, and models of coaching and can assist in the articulation of organizational goals will ensure that coaching programs align with the overarching organizational strategy.

I invite you to not stop at implementing coaching in your organization alone. Instead, imagine with me the future possibilities for coaching as it relates beyond organizations. Invite your mind to consider a world in which coaching helps us all learn and grow together, eventually unleashing the human potential of individuals, organizations, and societies around the globe.

"Living life is a choice. Making a difference in someone else's isn't."

—KID CUDI, RAPPER, SINGER, SONGWRITER, RECORD PRODUCER, AND ACTOR

CHAPTER SUMMARY: AT A GLANCE

- Because of the power of coaching to enhance the capability of learning and growth, coaching can help organizations and societies thrive in change in the coming years.

- Consulting firms, technology firms, communications firms, and recruiting firms are just a few examples of organizations that are successfully integrating coaching into their products and services to enhance product superiority and customer loyalty.

- The ICF Foundation's mission is to "Connect and equip professional coaches and organizations to accelerate and amplify impact on social progress through coaching." Its efforts are catalyzing the work of mission-driven organizations around the globe.

- The possibilities for coaching in the future are only limited by our imaginations. I invite you to join me in the collective approach to learning and growing together to build a better global society.

APPENDIX

For more training, templates, and resources visit:
www.corecompetenciesofchange.com.

ENDNOTES

1   International Coaching Federation, "ICF 2020 Global Coaching Study," accessed June 15, 2021, https://coachingfederation.org/research/global-coaching-study.

2   International Coaching Federation, "ICF 2020 Global Coaching Study," accessed June 15, 2021, https://coachingfederation.org/research/global-coaching-study.

3   PR Newswire, "US Tech Employment Surpasses 12 Million Workers, Accounts for 10% of Nation's Economy," accessed June 15, 2021, https://www.prnewswire.com/news-releases/us-tech-employment-surpasses-12-million-workers-accounts-for-10-of-nations-economy-301044415.html#:~:text=At%20%241.9%20trillion%2C%20the%20tech,adding%20%24745.5%20billion%20in%20output.

4   PR Newswire, "US Tech Employment Surpasses 12 Million Workers, Accounts for 10% of Nation's Economy," accessed June 15, 2021, https://www.prnewswire.com/news-releases/us-tech-employment-surpasses-12-million-workers-accounts-for-10-of-nations-economy-301044415.html#:~:text=At%20%241.9%20trillion%2C%20the%20tech,adding%20%24745.5%20billion%20in%20output.

5   Peter Salovey and John D. Mayer, "Emotional Intelligence," accessed June 15, 2021, https://journals.sagepub.com/doi/abs/10.2190/DUGG-P24E-52WK-6CDG?journalCode=icaa#:~:text=This%20article%20presents%20a%20framework,and%20achieve%20in%20one's%20life.

6   Daniel Goleman, "Emotional Intelligence," accessed June 15, 2021, https://www.danielgoleman.info/books/emotional-intelligence/.

7   Ronald A. Heifetz, "The Practice of Adaptive Leadership," accessed June 15, 2021, https://www.amazon.com/Practice-Adaptive-Leadership-Changing-Organization-ebook/dp/B004OC071W.

8   Stanford Business, "2013 Executive Coaching Survey," accessed June 15, 2021, https://www.gsb.stanford.edu/faculty-research/publications/2013-executive-coaching-survey.

9   Peter Senge, "The Fifth Discipline," accessed June 15, 2021, https://www.amazon.com/Fifth-Discipline-Practice-Learning-Organization-ebook/dp/B000SEIFKK/ref=sr_1_1?dchild=1&keywords=the+fifth+discipline&qid=1615996700&s=digital-text&sr=1-1.

10   Carol S. Dweck, "Mindset: The New Psychology of Success," accessed June 15, 2021, https://www.amazon.com/Mindset-Psychology-Carol-S-Dweck/dp/0345472322.

11   *Psychology Today*, "What Is Therapy?" accessed June 15, 2021, https://www.psychologytoday.com/us/basics/therapy.

12   Robert Kegan, "Immunity to Change," accessed June 15, 2021, https://www.amazon.com/Immunity-Change-Potential-Organization-Leadership/dp/1422117367.

13   International Coaching Federation, "ICF Code of Ethics," accessed June 15, 2021, https://coachingfederation.org/ethics/code-of-ethics.

14   International Coaching Federation, "ICF Foundation Strategic Plans," accessed June 15, 2021, https://foundationoficf.org/icf-foundation-strategic-plans/.

15   International Coaching Federation, "Coaching for Good: Ignite's Impact Story," accessed June 15, 2021, https://vimeo.com/412904730.

16   United Nations Foundation, accessed June 15, 2021, https://unfoundation.org/.

17   UNESCO Institute for Statistics, "Out of School Children and Youth," accessed June 15, 2021, http://uis.unesco.org/en/topic/out-school-children-and-youth.

18   ICF Foundation, "Engaging Coaching for Humanity and the Planet," accessed June 15, 2021, https://foundationoficf.org/engage/ignite/.

19   "Ignite: ICF Bulgaria," Vimeo, accessed June 15, 2021, https://vimeo.com/383824948.

20   "Ignite: ICF Oman," Vimeo, accessed June 15, 2021, https://vimeo.com/383825591.

21   "Ignite: ICF Bulgaria," Vimeo, accessed June 15, 2021, https://vimeo.com/383824948.

22   "Ignite: ICF Costa Rica," Vimeo, accessed June 15, 2021, https://vimeo.com/383825109.

ACKNOWLEDGMENTS

Thanks to:

Diane Stewart, the best sister and manuscript reviewer, and my reviewers and colleagues: Kathy Taberner, Bob Fleshner, Dr. Christopher Currens, Susan Braverman, Vicki Weisman, Elizabeth Stewart, and my editor, Rachel Hartman

Those who shared their stories and their wisdom: Dr. Philipia Hillman, Dr. Tatjana Dragovic Andersen, Janet Harvey, Morel Fourman, Anthony Stamilio, Hope Needham, Christopher Brookfield, Lisa Banks, Kevin Kruse, Nick Halder, Jenna Filipkowski, Renee Robertson, Coura Badiane, Ali Bahrami, Franziska Weiss, Cathy Maginelli, Alejandro Campos Cerda, Dr. Cathy Bush

And of course, to all those friends and family who keep me sane every day

ABOUT THE AUTHOR

Sandi has been an executive coach and consultant in hundreds of organizations for over twenty years with her company, SLS Coaching & Consulting. She has been an adjunct professor of leadership development at the University of Maryland's business school and a coach instructor for ICF- and ACTP-accredited coach training programs at American University and George Mason University. She reviews ethics cases around the world as a member of the International Coach Federation Independent Review Board. She received her BA from Colgate University and an MBA from Columbia University Business School. She worked for international companies including Johnson & Johnson and Ferrero N.A., where she managed new products. She has two children and three stepchildren and lives with her husband in Washington, DC. She skis, bikes, hikes, and does yoga whenever possible.